MY F**K-IT

LIST

BARRY M. FEIST

Copyright-2015, by Barry M. Feist

ISBN- 978-0-9733184-7-0

Other books by the author, both in hard-copy and e-book:

WRECK-A-MENDED REEDING

DEAR GABBY

CHICKEN SOOP FOR DUMB-EEZ

O-BITCH-UARIES

CLASS-IF-EYED ADS

Website- WRITINGS-R-ME.COM
Blog;   barrymfeist.com

A HAT'S OFF

To all the good, kind-hearted, people, who work with, and for, the better treatment of animals.

Organizations such as:

The Society For The Prevention of Cruelty to Animals, in the various countries they operate in.

The Humane Societies around the globe.

All the veterinarians who devote their time free of charge, and the many private individuals who assist animals in need.

It's a good thing for the millions of mistreated or uncared for animals, that there are such people and organizations out there to assist them.

Humans have to be the voice for those that can't speak.

INTRODUCTION

If you were to ask a mountain climber, why he climbs mountains, likely as not, he would reply; "Because they're there".

If you asked a bank robber why he robs banks, likely as not he would reply, "Because, that's where the money is."

Both, straight forward, and simplistic answers, albeit, not necessarily rational nor logical. But, I can accept that. I like things simplistic in life. I don't like a lot of complications, I hate making dates or commitments. I just like life to carry on as it's supposed to. Certainly hurdles and problems are thrown at us, as we journey down the path of life, but, we shouldn't go looking for them.

If I wanted complexity in life, I would give a second look at the formula Einstein used to come up with his; 'Theory of Relativity'. Who knows, maybe he got it wrong. Maybe he forgot to take six to the fourth-power, or forgot to carry a one. But, before I tackled that, I'd first have to look up how to spell Einstein, meaning; are the latter vowels; 'ei', or 'ie'? Turns out, they are as I positioned them; 'ei'.

Everybody has goals. Nothing wrong with that, providing, they're attainable and logical. If you're a mute, the chances of you becoming a famous orator or singer are almost nil. If you only have one leg, the chances of you becoming a World Olympic Ass Kicker are less than one percent. And , the list goes on.

At one time, perhaps, when, as Billy Joel sang; "When I wore a younger man's clothes", I probably had a few things on my bucket list. Now, that I'm into my twilight years, still wearing a younger man's clothes, that don't fit so well anymore, there are more things I don't want to do, than things I want to do.

So, just as people make up, 'Bucket Lists' to remind them what they want to accomplish in life, I've made up a 'F- -k It List' to let myself, and everyone else, know things I have no intention of ever doing nor even trying.

WATER PERILS

Water; tasteless, colorless, and odorless. Be pretty hard to live without it, even impossible. Personally, I don't really drink it, at least not in its raw state, as I don't know how many contaminants are in it, and, if there's one thing I don't like in my drinks, it's contaminants.

The water for making beer is boiled, thus killing any contaminants, thus, making it safe to drink , even for babies. I like beer, and drink, not only my share, but the share of half a dozen other people as well. Not just for the health reasons, but, just because I can.

We need water for other things such as: cooking, bathing and cleaning. The oceans, rivers and lakes, all made up of water; provide mankind with recreation, travel and livelihoods.

Now, it's all fine and dandy to enjoy and use water responsibly, but, to challenge it, that's going a bit too far, for my liking. Following are some examples, of pushing the water envelope.

WHITE-WATER RAFTING

First off, for those of you who are landlubbers, water is only white, when it is angry and agitated.

Think of the agitator in your washing machine. Same principle; a force is agitating the water. Water does not like to be agitated, and when it is, it, turns white. Agitated water, with the exception of being in your washing machine, is generally not a good thing.

I don't care how much I've had to drink, how many chicks there are to impress, if I see white, agitated water, I steer clear of it.

Calm water, I can handle that. Calm water is soothing, and tranquil. I like calm water. Calm water is my friend. But, agitated water, forget about it. That scares the hell out of me, and I don't want to be around it.

Even when I do laundry, I quickly throw my clothes in the machine and take a powder, before the water starts agitating.

Here's me: I get in a small boat, usually made of; wood, fibreglass or aluminum. I find a tranquil piece of water, and slowly paddle around at a leisurely pace, enjoying nature, all the while, also enjoying the dozen or so beer, I have in my cooler.

I have on my life jacket, in the event, I should get pulled into the water by a rogue marlin, shark, or whale, or accidentally fall in, whilst trying to retrieve a beer I drop overboard.

That's enjoying water. That's like saying to the water; "Hey water. I'm just here to enjoy your calmness, and have no intentions of agitating you. Let's be friends. Don't get agitated, and turn white."

And, in so doing, the water says calm and tranquil. It does not get agitated and turn white, and water and I are good. We're both at peace with nature and the world.

Here's a white water rafter: he gets into a *rubber* boat, goes down fast-flowing rapids, gets tossed about, quite possibly causing some sort of brain displacement, and, if he doesn't drown, will probably bash his stupid head against some sharp rocks.

Now, he doesn't do this alone. No. He has a bunch of other knuckleheads, he's convinced to come with him, by plying them with booze. Then, they all think they're master sailors, and off they go, likely as not, with some females in tow. Just goes to show you, not only men are stupid.

These characters will shoot down these rapids, paddling and yelling, swaying to and fro, like there's no tomorrow, all in order to try to make it out alive and, to dry land.

Newsflash. Why not stay on dry land, in the first place, then you don't have to risk your life, trying to get on it, in the second place.

Apparently, there's even 'special 'white water trips for seniors. Yeah, I'm up for that. I'll just take my walker and set it in the raft, then, strap my oxygen tank to the side, and, away I go.

The only way I'd take a rafting trip, whether I'm a senior or not, is; if I started at the bottom of the rapids, where the water is calm, and watch as those mucho dudes try to paddle up river. Not going to happen.

There are all sorts of ways my life might come to an end" perhaps I'll have a heart attack; maybe I'll be in a ten-scooter pile-up at some seniors function; I could fall and break my hip, and get some sort of infection. However, one way I know I'm not going to be checking out, and that's while white-water rafting.

Are you apt to see me white water rafting? Not hardly, unless they have such a venue at Disneyland, and I can grab on to some young kid to keep myself from drowning, even if I have to drown him or her in the process.

So, I'm going to float white-water rafting; on my F**k- It List. Just where it belongs.

SURFING

Yeah. This appeals to me. Again with the agitated water, but, this time, it's literally over your head, and you have to move fast enough ahead of it, or it can crush or drown you. But, believe it or not, there's more to it than that.

Before you get out to the part of the ocean where you want to start your-surf run, or; "catch a wave", as they say, you have to sit on your surfboard, and hand-paddle your sorry ass out to the middle of the friggin' ocean. How un-fun is that?

Let's just say *you* were under the water, seeing these feet and hands thrashing about, and, let's just say, you were a shark. What do you think your reaction as a shark would be?

Hungry, angry shark, sees these KFC-type drumsticks moving about in the water. What's the shark thinking? "Lunchtime. I didn't even have to order in, they delivered. Cool. I like this section of the ocean."

14

What's the Dude thinking? "After this run, I'm going to go in and eat, I'm hungry. Maybe I'll go in and have some fish for lunch." Which, or, whom, do you think is going to have lunch first?

If the surfer dude's lucky, and I mean real lucky, when, and if, he gets back to shore, he'll only have a partial board left, and a shark's dental impression on the remaining part. If he's not so lucky, he'll have the shark's dental impression on what's left of his leg.

The only consolation I can see in being a surfer-dude, is that I might meet some nice chicks on the beach. However, I don't know how many chicks are into one-legged, or one-armed surfers, so the chick thing probably isn't worth the shark thing.

I think I'd just as soon go up and down the beach, looking for ninety-eight pound weaklings, and kick sand in their faces.

Wanting to be a surfer-dude, is so on my F**k-It List.

SCUBA DIVING

Under the surface of the water, live all sorts
of dangerous: animals, reptiles; mammals;
and what have you. That's why they're
under the water, and not on land. Thus, since
they don't come on to the land, I have
decided I won't go under the water. Their
turf, my turf, as it were.

First off, humans cannot breathe under water
without the proper equipment. That, in itself,
should be a pretty good indicator, that
humans do not belong under water.

Why is it, some people always want to go,
where they're not supposed to? It's like
telling a little kid not to do something, and
they go and do it in spite. Or putting a sign
up not to open a door or touch such and
such, and sure enough, someone will open
that door or touch the item.

Why can't we accept the fact there are just
some places we don't belong, and were
never meant to go to, or be in?

First off, you are in the water under artificial circumstances, vis a vis an oxygen tank.

You never see fish on land using a water tank to support them, whilst they are trying to be like humans. No. Fish know their place, and that place is in and under the water. Just as a human's place is out of, and above, the water.

Why would a person even think about going under the water? You don't belong there, anymore than you belong in the sky, like a bird.

So they make scuba equipment which allows a person go under the water. Does that mean you have to use it? They also make bullet-proof vests. Does that mean you want people to shoot at you? I doubt it.

Going under the water, and risk the possibility of drowning, or being eaten by a shark of a killer whale, is way up there, on my F**k -It List. And I don't expect it to come down any time soon.

TAKE AN OCEAN CRUISE

I, as well as most people I know, are what
are referred to as; "Landlubbers." We grew
up on the prairies, where the closest ocean
was hundreds of miles away, and that's
where it belonged.

Sure, we have water on the prairies, but, in
the form of sloughs, creeks, lakes and rivers.
And, while on any one of these, I can still
see, and am not far from, good old terra
firma.

On the prairies, you can always see into the
distance and see something different, be it
hills, trees, houses, what have you. And, if
you turn and look in another direction, the
whole scene can change.

Not so on an ocean. On an ocean, no matter
in which direction you're facing, all you see
is more ocean, and lots of it.

What I know of the ocean, is what I've read
in books, seen on TV, or from stories related
to me by people who have been on one.

Thus, I don't understand why people want to take ocean cruises. Did they not hear about the Titanic? That was supposed to be state-of-the art, but, things didn't end up well for that boat.

To me, a cruise ship is nothing more than a glorified floating hotel. I would never stay locked in a hotel with several thousand people, for days or weeks on end. Why would I do so on a ship, that's in the middle of the ocean, with no escape?

Maybe they're trying to live vicariously, through some old romantic movie they saw, whereby a couple fell in love on a cruise and would stand on deck and look at the stars. Maybe they want to stand on the bow, and yell; "I'm the king of the world". I don't know.

Getting seasick is quite common with people on cruise ships. So, wanting to spend two weeks puking, being confined with a bunch of dorky strangers, on a vessel that could capsize and toss me into shark-infested waters, is definitely an adventure that would be on my F**k-It List.

GO OVER NIAGARA FALLS IN A BARREL

Almost since the Niagara Falls were discovered, many years ago, there has always been some foolhardy person who wanted to go over them in a barrel. This, I have never understood.

What's the point here? Let's just say you do it, and succeed, which a few, very few, people have done. How did that venture enhance your life, or make you a better person?

Would this feat set the stage for you to get into a particular line of work? Would it further your career-goals having stated on your résumé that you went over Niagara Falls?

Why do people risk their lives for a fleeting minute of fame? I don't get that. Who out there, goes to Niagara Falls, and rather than enjoying the beauty and wonder of it, say to themselves; " Hey, this is okay to look at, but, how cool would it be to go over those Falls in a barrel, or some other such contraption."

What if, you were a person who decided to go over the Falls, were secured in a barrel and set afloat. But, a few minutes into it, you decided that maybe this wasn't such a good idea, and that you might want to live to see how the ending to that murder mystery in that book you were reading turned out?

At this stage, while floating closer to the Falls, your options are nonexistent. You have no recourse to contact someone and tell them that you've changed your mind.

That would be my biggest fear. Sure, I might attempt to do this on a dare, or after a few martini vodkas with beer chasers. but, once I was actually in the barrel, and the booze wore off, it's a little late to have second-thoughts.

I'd be thinking whilst in the barrel; "Okay, if I survive this, what will I have accomplished? What if the barrel breaks, and I end up with a bunch of splinters in my ass, that can't be good. Thus, barrelling over Niagara Falls, goes on my F**k-It List.

SWIM WITH THE GREAT WHITES

I've never seen a Great White up close. Or, at a distance, for that matter. And, I'd prefer to keep it that way.

However, I've watched enough nature shows to know, without any firsthand experience, that Great Whites, although in the fish-type family, as are sardines, are not to be trifled with. The Great Whites, not the sardines. I have absolutely no fear of sardines whatsoever. Let me be clear about that.

People who have a lot more courage and curiosity than I, seem to find it adventurous and exciting to swim with sharks. To me, this is no different than going in the baboons', or, lions' cage at a zoo, and taunting them. That wouldn't turn out well.

I'm guessing that sharks are like me; they don't particularly like strangers on their turf. Especially, when the strangers want to get up close and personal, by petting them.

I'm also guessing, if sharks wanted to be petted by humans, they'd swim up to shore or to a pier, like dolphins do.

Sharks have big teeth, and they can eat just about anything they want, especially humans. So, with that in mind, why would anyone want to mess with them?

Sure, I've heard all the rhetoric from shark experts, whereby a shark will very seldom attack a human, but, what if I'd the exception?

I don't know when the shark last ate, or what kind of a mood it's in, nor do I particularly want to find out.

If I wanted to be close to some animal in the wild, in its own habitat, I'd probably pick a rabbit or a gopher. Same thing, as far as I'm concerned, they're animals in the wild. It's just with the latter, my life isn't in peril, and, if it attacks me, I can probably kill it with one good swift kick to the head. That's what I'm talking about.

With a shark, I have almost a zero chance of defeating it in its own turf, or water, in this case. It has the clear advantage. I like to have the, 'edge', as it were. Swimming with Great Whites, or even average Whites, is so on my F**k-It List.

GO WHALE-WATCHING

Environmentalists, animals lovers, earth and sea people and, just regular tourists, are into this outdoorsy pastime.

To be an active participant in this little venture, you will be doing so with a certain amount of risk to your life. Not real great risk, mind you, but an amount, which is, more than I am willing to take. Especially, considering the end result. That being: seeing a big damn fish in the wild. Big whoop.

Fish look quite good when lined up in a small can, ground up in a small can, or wrapped in ice in my supermarket.

The desire to go out and watch whales eludes me. There are all sorts of little teeny-tiny fish that live in the ocean, and seeing one of those is a one-in-a-million chance, but, no one seems to want to.

Even an octopus is not that common of a sight, or, a sea horse. However, these rare sea animals don't seem to interest the general population of aquatic life-lovers.

24

No. Whale watchers want to go out onto the sea, and look for these fish, that are literally the size of a Sherman tank. And, when they see one, or perhaps several, it is a big thrill, even a life-changing event for them.

Are you kidding me? How can you not see these things? And, why would you want to? I'm guessing once you've seen one whale, you've seen them all. Go to one of those water parks where they have whales in captivity, have a good look at it, take a few photos, and call that good for the rest of your life.

I've seen some news or documentary film footage whereby people have gotten too close to a whale, and it capsized their boat, and sometimes even crushed it, if the whale jumped out of the water and landed on it.

Who would want to risk losing a good boat, or your life, for that matter, just to see a whale? Not me. That's who not. If the whale wants me to watch it, it can damn well swim close to shore, and let out one of its whale calls. Short of that happening, whale-watching, goes on my F**k-It List.

DO A POLAR BEAR PLUNGE

For those unknowing, this is an event held in various countries, but, mostly in Canada. Basically, it is just for crazy fun, oftentimes by those three sheets to the wind, but , as is the case in parts of Canada, it can also be a venue to raise money for the Special Olympics.

What is entailed here is; for people to don their swim suits, or not, and, in the middle of winter, go to a lake, river or ocean, that is somewhat free of ice, and jump into the freezing water.

If this sounds like a stupid thing to do, that's exactly what it is. Now, believe it or not, this is even somewhat of a competitive sport.

The people who raise the most money can go on to plunge into another bigger, possibly, colder lake, river or ocean. Perhaps there's even some sort of prize such as a year's free therapy with some southern Shrink, I don't know.

But; 'Wow', what a goal that would be, not only to set your sites on, but, to achieve. What is it with people wanting to go to such extremes, and jump into frigid waters?

Hypothermia. Have these crazy fools never heard of that? It's a condition whereby you get so cold that your body temperature drops, and you can literally die.

Why would a person want to risk their life, just for some silly event that some numb-skull dreamed up whilst in a drunken stupor, and he or she, fell into a frigid lake?

I don't even like it if my shower water is too cool. Perhaps my wife had a bath prior to my shower, and she used up most of the hot water. I almost go ballistic is she does this, knowing that she will use one hundred gallons of hot water, just to wash her hair.

So, with all this in mind, I'm going to go out in public, on a cold winter day and plunge into a body of frigid water. Not hardly.

Polar Bear Plunging is a F**k-It List item.

LEARN HOW TO SWIM

Unlike fishermen on an ocean, prairie people really don't have to know how to swim, unless they join some community pool, have a slough, lake, or river near, or on, their property.

Therefore, I have never learned how swim. Yes, on one or two occasions in my life, I gave swimming a feeble attempt. However, on those occasions, I generally sank to the bottom and got a mouth full of water. Neither experience being a positive one, encouraging me to keep trying.

That said, I know a lot of people, including my own children who can swim. They seem to have a lot of fun doing it. Going to lakes, pools, water slides, what have you.

I'll watch as people swim about in pools or lakes , and ask myself; "does that look like fun? Would I like to do that?" And, every time the answer comes back; a resounding, "No."

Humans do not belong in water, with the exception of a hot tub or bathtub.

I wonder if fish look at humans and say to themselves; " WTF. Why are there humans in my hood? They don't have fins or gills. We don't go on land and try to catch them or walk around them and take photos, so why do they do it to us?"

Humans are always going where they don't belong. We belong on land, not in the water. If were supposed to be in those places, we'd have fins and gills.

I could see advantages to me learning to swim: I could go underwater, and grab other swimmers by the leg, and scare the hell out of them. Maybe, if someone I liked fell in the water and couldn't swim, I could possibly jump in and save them. Or, save even a stranger for that matter, providing I'd be given 'hero' status, or some cash reward.

Other than that, I see no reason for learning how to swim. I'll just wash away that idea, and put learning to swim, on my F**k-It List.

AIR PERILS

I like air. I'm sure it would be quite difficult to try to get along without it. How could you blow up a balloon without air? How could you blow out birthday candles, or even light them, for that matter, without air? And, more importantly, how could they put the fizz in beer without air? So you see, air is a necessary commodity.

Now, I don't know exactly how much air there is out there. Don't know how they measure it, nor do I know anyone who does, and could care less. Are we slowly running out of it, like oil? Or, is air self-replenishing?

There are fewer things I know about air, than things I do know about it. However, the one thing I do know is; I like to have more air above me, than below me. Meaning, I prefer to stay planted on terra firma.

Thus, I really don't like being too high up in the air, with the exception of being in a plane, and even that isn't a thrill for me. But, being *in* a plane is a lot more appealing to me, than jumping out of one. I get vertigo just from standing on a bath mat.

SKYDIVING

You've got to wonder who first came up
with the concept of jumping out of a plane,
and why. Why did some guy get the idea to
leave the plane? Why didn't he just wait
until it landed? After all, you don't jump out
of a moving bus or train, before you reach
your destination, so why would you a plane?

When you take skydiving lessons,
apparently on your first few jumps, you're
strapped to an expert. This entails having
him harnessed to your back. Imagine how
that would look if you both hit the ground.

Not a sight I'd want in my family's photo
album. If I take swimming lessons, I don't
have a guy strapped to my back, nor with
skiing, or golfing lessons, so what's the deal
here?

I can only assume that the skydiving school
operates much like any business; they want
to get the cheapest product available so they
can make the largest profit.

Thus, I envision the skydiving school buying used sheets, possibly purchased for ten cents on the dollar, at a Ku Klux Klan flea market, and, having some little old lady sew them together with factory-defect thread. Her not taking the time to sew over the eye slots, thus making the chutes less aero-dynamic.

I can't comprehend the first person to try out a parachute. You're looking at risking your life on a bunch of used sheets sewn together.

You're already flying through the air in the airplane, leave it at that. If you want air, open a window, but, don't jump out.

Why would a sane person even contemplate such a move? I wouldn't even jump off a kitchen chair, let alone, jump out of an airplane.

What if your chute doesn't open, and, you realize this while still a mile above the earth? Regrets and second thoughts won't be of any use to you then.

Skydiving; is high on my F**k -It List. And there is no pun intended.

TAKE AN EXPLORATORY SPACE FLIGHT

Technology being what it is today, we can literally send men into outer space. And, not only governments, with their vast taxpayer wealth, can do this, but, more and more, individuals, albeit, rich ones, can do this.

Right now there are two private citizens, with their own companies, who are both trying to get a private space-ship built, that will take citizens into outer space and back.

What's the incentive here? People say; "I want to be a pioneer". Okay. Get yourself a covered wagon, and head across the U.S. Midwest, to California, then build your wife, and youngins, a log cabin.

God put us on this earth, and He probably figured we'd go snooping around and discovering other countries and things on this earth. He's probably cool with that.

However, I think that if He would have wanted us to leave this earth, He'd have built some sort of stairs or ladders, to do so.

Going into space, is big-time dangerous, as past episodes have revealed. Astronauts were almost stuck behind the moon, and, shuttles blew up after take-off.

I can just imagine what it would be like to be stuck in space. It's not like you can call Triple A. You'd be going around and around the earth, like the Griswalds in a London round-about, maybe even spot your house, but, there wasn't a damn thing you could do, and no one could get you back. Bummer.

It would be like on a carousel and as you went around, your family and friends would wave to you, but they could never talk to, nor touch you again. And then one time you came around, and you'd be dead.

What is it people want to see, or experience by going into space? You can see how the earth looks by looking at video from the Space Station.

I don't have to be hit by a bus to know it will severely hurt me, if not in fact, kill me. I'm okay letting someone else take the chances, and risk, or lose their life. Going into outer space goes on my, F**k –It List.

WING-SUITING

This little hobby, or sport, is similar, in some respects, to skydiving, except, that you do this off a mountain, and with a suit made to resemble a big wing.

Essentially, you jump off a cliff, then open your arms, and this wing-suit you have on, allows you to fly, kind of.

You're going about a hundred miles an hour heading towards the earth, and, at the last moment, open a parachute. Wow. How invigorating that must be. Not.

First off, you're relying on the fact that this wing-suit was made properly, and that it will carry you aloft for the allotted time. Second, you will hope that you don't crash into a mountainside, and, if you don't, that you can deploy your chute, and flow gently to the ground. A lot of factors to think about, as you're plummeting towards earth, and certain death, if things should go wrong.

Let's just say that your suit doesn't perform as the guarantee said it would, and now, instead on heading towards the earth at one hundred-miles an hour, you're travelling double that speed.

First question you'll be asking yourself as the earth gets closer is; "Maybe I should not have gotten this discount wing-suit, and spent the extra coin for the premium model."

Next, you'll be asking yourself, as the earth is now a lot closer, and you deploy your chute; "I bought this chute at the same discount store, as the wing-suit, how is it going to work out for me?

Well pilgrims, at this stage it's a little too late of worry about things like that, as you're starting to get close enough to the ground to indentify insects.

Hopefully, your chute will open. If not, you can strike this adventure off your bucket list.

Wing-suiting, goes on my F**k-It List, to be sure.

BUNGEE JUMPING

As with the parachute, who would have first
tested a bungee cord, and why? Does a
trampoline not serve the same purpose?

Why in god's name would a person jump off
a one-hundred foot bridge, almost hit the
bottom, and then be pulled back to dangle
up and down for a while?

Is it a case where you want to see if all your
brain cells will fall back into place by the
sudden jolt at the bottom?

Who stands on the top of a high precipice
and looks down, thinking; "I'd like to jump
down there, but, not quite hit the bottom and
be pulled back up"?

Who does not see the possible flaws in this
venture? Do you really think the guys who
operate this business buy the top-of-the-line
bungees?

If you're jumping off a bridge spanning a
river, do they allow for the rising or
lowering of the water, depending on the
season or rainfall? Should they not?

How many times in your life have you snapped an elastic band, whether on purpose or by accident? Not all that hard to do. So, then why would you put your life in the hands of a big elastic band-maker? After all, that's all a bungee cord is; a great big elastic band.

Just what is going through your miniature little brain as you stand atop a high structure looking down, hoping that the guy who measured the bungee cord isn't dyslexic, and, out by a foot or two, and hoping the past-due date isn't up on the cord, and will last one more jump.

As we all know, things wear out. Just how many jumps can you get out of one bungee cord? Are you the last one? Is there an expiry date on the bungee cord, or, at the very least, the number of jumps it will be able to sustain? Did you look at it to see where you stand in the pecking order?

On my F**k-It List, that's where bungee jumping belongs. And, I'm placing it at the bottom with no chance of coming back up.

HOT-AIR BALLOONING

How safe can this be? You're standing in a
basket made out of wicker, a very
combustion able material, and just a few feet
above you is a set of propane tanks belching
out flames into a plastic, or vinyl, giant-
sized balloon. Hello. Does that not have
disaster written all over it, or is it just me?

I have some lawn furniture made out of
wicker, and, one day, whilst in a drunken
stupor, spilled some brandy on it, and while
trying to light my cigar, set the whole damn
set ablaze.

Let me tell you, that set didn't last too long.
Went up like a cotton field in Georgia
during the Civil War.

I had to do some smooth talking when my
wife came home. Blamed it on lightning, or
on the kids, I don't remember, but, that's
another story.

At any rate, if I'm going to be dangling a
thousand feet above the earth, I'd prefer it to
be in a fire-proof enclosure. Especially when
I have a fifty-foot flame above me.

How is it that people find this an adventure? The cost of an air balloon ride can run upwards of one hundred dollars. Unbelievable. You'd pay some stranger a C-Note to put your life in danger? Not me.

With hot-air ballooning, you have to go with the wind. Meaning, it doesn't matter in what direction you want to go, you have no choice. You are going to go in the direction the wind is blowing.

How much sense does that make? You wouldn't get in a car that relied solely on wind and hope that it would take you in the direction you wanted to go.

No. You want to go in a certain direction, by choice or necessity. But, with a hot-air balloon, you do not have that option.

Why anyone would take a mode of transport, that will take them in any random direction, while at the same time, risking their life doing so, is beyond me.

Put hot-air ballooning on my F**k-It List.

HANG GLIDING

Hang gliding is a sport whereby you have a contraption, not unlike a big giant triangle, attached to a big kite, and hook yourself up , and, jump off high places. Then, you soar through the air like a big bird.

You do not need any experience to hang-glide. As I see it, all you have to be able to do is, temporarily, defy the law of gravity. I've done that by swinging on my kids' backyard swing. No big deal there.

I defy gravity every day, all day long, just by staying upright when I walk. Of course, there have been occasions when gravity gets the upper hand and I fall down, but, by and large, I've pretty much, through years of experience, got that gravity-defying thing, down to a science.

That is providing, I stay as close to terra firma as possible. Once I decide to take my chances, and leave solid ground, albeit for a few seconds, gravity always wins.

I'm not afraid of heights, providing they're above me. For example, I can look up at a tall building or mountain, and it has no affect on me. I do not get dizzy nor experience vertigo.

However, if that is reversed, meaning I am high up, and everything else is low-down, that is another matter. I am not comfortable with that. When I am high up, I know I have to eventually, be it slowly or quickly, go down.

If I'm at the top of a mountain in my car, and driving down, that's okay, as I will take my time getting down. However, if I am standing on a cliff and jump off, using a kite-like contraption, I know that I will be going down at a speed that gravity, the wind, my weight , and the big kite, dictates.

Not comfortable in that zone. I have no problem flying a kite, when I'm on the ground, and the kite is in the sky. However, I am not keen on hanging *on* the kite.

Thus, hang-gliding is another anti-gravity, air thing on my F**k -It List.

OTHER LIFE PERILS

By and large, life itself, can be perilous, just in the everyday things.

You can get injured at work. Say, you're sitting at your desk, and while folding some papers, you get the dreaded and painful, paper cut, and, end up in traction.

Perhaps your secretary, or some other minion you have working for you, brings you your morning coffee, and spills it in your lap, thereby scalding your private parts.

Maybe you operate some big piece of machinery, and while climbing into it, you scrape or bang your knee.

Out on the road, on your way to or from work, there are all sorts of women drivers, and we all know what a highway hazard they can be.

Perhaps while driving, and talking on your cell phone, you become distracted, and slam into some damn fool who's stopped at a; red light. That can cause serious injury.

And, the list goes on. Here's more.

GO MOUNTAIN CLIMBING

'Because they're there'. That's what the mountain-climbing folks will tell you is the reason they climb mountains.

That's their only reason? Just what the hell would these people be doing if there were no mountains?

Would they just be sitting around the house and their wife would tell them to take out the trash, and they would say: "Why"? And the wife would say; "Because it's there." And he'd say; "That doesn't make a whole lot of sense".

Climbing the average, or more to the point, above average, mountain, is no small feat. It can take months of planning, involve tens of thousands of dollars, and several dozen people.

The whole thing has to be planned very precise. They don't just hike up a big mountain in one day, but, in several, and, by doing it in stages.

The ultimate goal for all mountain climbers is to scale Everest. The tallest mountain on the planet at over twenty-nine thousand feet. Higher than a lot of planes fly.

In my view, a mountain is not there to climb, but rather, to go around, or through, as the case may be. If a mountain is in your way, take another route.

The perils in climbing a mountain, especially one like Everest, are phenomenal. Literally hundreds of people have perished trying to conquer it.

Knowing this, why would you even try? Would you not look at the statistics and say to yourself; "Screw this nonsense. I could get killed climbing a mountain, and, for what, just to show off to my girlfriend.?"

I'm staying on the flat prairies where I belong. If I have the urge to climb something, I'll climb up an anthill , or on the roof of my garden shed.

Climbing mountains just climbed on to my F**k-It List.

HELI-SKIING, or, DOWN-HILL SKIING

First off, I'm not a skier. Not, downhill, cross country, nor cross-hill and down-country. Skiing involves being in the snow, and cold, and, I detest both.

Fine and dandy. However, before you ski *down* a mountain, you first have to get to the *top* of the mountain. To do so, a person can take a ski lift or tram up a mountain.

However, there are some; 'avid' skiers, who are not satisfied with this activity, and choose to push the envelope. By that I mean, they want to go off the beaten path, via a helicopter, get dropped off on top of some obscure mountain, and ski down it.

First off, heli' is a derivative of helicopter, but closer to the term, 'hell', as that 's what you can be going through. Think about it. You're going to a spot so remote that it is only accessible by helicopter. Shouldn't that be telling you something right there? Like, perhaps you don't belong there in the first place.

If something should happen, such as an avalanche or you fall and break you stupid leg, it could be a long time until help arrives.

Why is going skiing with a helicopter better than at a regular resort? Sure, you like the virgin-fresh powder. But, where I come from snow is snow. It's white and slippery. How much more whiter or slipperier do you need it, that you'd risk your life for it?

As I stated, I'm not a skier, never have been, never intend to be. But, if I was one, I can pretty much guarantee you I would not be so fanatical about it that I would want to hire a helicopter to take me to some desolate mountain-top, hours and miles away from civilization, just to get some fresh powder.

When it comes to snow, I'm satisfied with the regular old used kind. I only like fresh when it comes to food, such as; beer; baked goods, meats and produce.

I wouldn't be that fussy or vain as to only want to ski on snow no one else has. What do I care who skied on the snow before me? As long as I'm safe. Heli-skiing, and downhill-skiing, go on my F**k-It List.

CROSS-COUNTRY SKIING

Canada, the country from which I hail, is a pretty big country. Matter of fact, it's the second largest on the planet. As of yet, and I'm talking some sixty-plus years, I have never driven across the entire country.

Therefore, I can't, for the life of me, see skiing across it. I'm guessing that cross-country skiing was thought-up by sports-minded folk who came from small countries such as; the Vatican or Monaco.

Perhaps I'm looking at this in the literal sense, when I should be looking at it in the virtual sense. People don't mean they want to actually ski across a country per se, but, rather, ski across part of it, while out in the countryside.

Regardless, whether the former or latter are true, what's the point? A person has to bear in mind, that unless you have someone to pick you up at the other end, however far you ski, you will have to ski that equal amount of distance back.

I can't even see me taking up downhill skiing, whereby I get a ride to the top, and let gravity take over, coming down. At least with this sport, sooner or later I end up at my initial starting point with little effort.

Essentially with cross-country skiing, you push yourself along with your ski poles as much as you move your feet. So, the health-starved individual might look at this as the glass half-full meaning; you get to exercise both your legs and your arms.

I, on the other hand, think the complete opposite, and see the glass half-empty. I see cross-country skiing, as tiring out both my arms and legs at the same time. Thus giving me no backup to get home once I've reached my max energy output, and, possibly perishing on the snow due to a stroke or cardiac arrest.

If the latter should happen, and I have to literally pull myself along the ground with my arms, or push with my legs as the case may be, I'd want to be in a small country.

So doing the cross-country skiing thingy would slide onto my F**k-It List.

RUN WITH THE BULLS

Bulls are big, mean, scary, and, usually very
ill-tempered. I have enough problem with
encountering one bull, let alone several.

In Pamplona, Spain, every year they have an
event they call; 'the running of the bulls'.
Essentially, what this entails is; a bunch of
angry bulls are turned loose in the streets,
and, people, in the streets are going to try to
outrun these bulls.

Who came up with that? And did he not see
that had 'disaster' written all over it? They
don't have a running of the lions or
elephants anyplace I know of, so why bulls?

I could maybe see a running of the squirrels,
or chipmunks or some such things, but
bulls?

What is the thrill here that I can't seem to
grasp? You're essentially running down a
street with a half-ton bovine coming behind
you that will run over you, and, possibly
gore you to death, with its horns, or both.

I can't help but wonder if some locals are caught off-guard during this event. Perhaps some guy was on a three-day drunk, and is just coming out of his house when he sees all these bulls coming toward him, and wonders if he's hallucinating.

Or, some tourists who just arrived and know nothing about this, are taking a casual stroll down a street, enjoying the day, when all of a sudden as they turn a corner, are confronted by a herd of angry bulls, and have no way to escape, but to run, with the bulls in hot pursuit. Put that vacation spot down as their first and last time.

Maybe the bullfighters instigated this event. Once the bulls have run for several blocks, and are all tired out, these, 'brave' bullfighters get into the arena, and taunt the bull. The bull that is by now so tired, it doesn't care whether it wins or loses the fight.

I possibly have enough courage that I could partake in a; 'running of the sheep'; or, ' running of the Shetland ponies' events. But, as for running with, by, or close to any mean bulls, that goes on my F**k-It List.

BE A STORM CHASER

Most people, and I'm one of them, go inside
when a storm approaches. If I should be
walking or driving, I'll try to avoid the storm
by going in the opposite direction. Not so
for Storm Chasers. These people run, *toward*
the storm.

I am not real keen on chasing things, unless,
maybe, if my hat blew off in the wind, I'd
chase that, for a while. Or, if during a
exceptionally high wind, a beautiful chick's
dress blew off, I'd chase that, but not as far
as I would my hat. I'd probably chase the
chick instead, but, you get my drift.

Storms tend to be unpredictable. They can
change course at the drop of a hat. I suppose
if a person, namely me, was one hundred-
percent sure the storm would always be
going in the direction opposite me, I could
act like a brave soul and chase it, if, for no
other reason, than to impress people.

Then, for a while, I'd be a, 'storm chaser',
but, if the storm reversed directions, I'd
quickly become a, 'storm chasee'.

I don't really know just how fast I can run, miles-per-hour, wise, but I can almost guarantee you, there isn't a storm or a tornado, I couldn't outrun.

Were I a Storm Chaser, if a storm was coming right at me, while I was hot-footing it in the opposite direction, I'd no doubt be asking myself why I was stupid enough to try such a venture in the first place. Also, I've no doubt that as I fled in panic, I'd be making all sorts of promises to God that if He spared me, I would never again attempt to do anything so foolhardy.

I know the Storm Chasers, chase storms for their livelihood and for scientific study. I'd like to know what they'd put on their job application when they first applied for such a job. Would they say that they just have a natural-gift to chase things?

How about life insurance? How hard would it be to get that if you told your agent that you deliberately risked your life for a living? You'd be paying top premiums, for that policy, I'm guessing.

Storm Chasing, goes on my F**k-It List.

55

TAKE A POLICE RIDE-A-LONG

From time to time, in different cities around the country, police will allow a ride-a-long. Usually for journalists, to see what police encounter in a typical day, night or week, as the case may be.

I'm guessing that the chances of a person getting injured or killed, while on the ride-a-long, are minimal. However, why take that chance?

The police get paid the big coin to risk, or give up their lives. I'm okay with that, but, for me to do it, I don't think so.

It would be just my luck, that I'd get in the car, that patrols the worst neighborhood, on the night, when there was a riot of some sort.

I'd probably end up in a Rodney King, or L.A. Riots type of thing. Or, there'd be some major event, that would cause all the local natives to go on the warpath, thereby putting my life in extreme peril.

I'm sure there's those out there who would find something like this thrilling, even, invigorating. Not me.

I'd wonder just how concerned the officers I'd ride with would be concerned about my well-being. They might have the same mindset as I do, whereby, I'd be saying; "Hey, if he wants to ride-along, he does so at his own risk. Be damned if I'm risking my life to save his, if things go down."

I could see going on a ride-a-long, if the police would provide me with; a bullet-proof vest, a taser; pepper spray; a 9mm Glock and a shotgun or AR15. To me, that would make a level playing field with the undesirable elements out there.

In this day and age, with body cameras and what have you, ride-a-longs have almost become obsolete, as a reporter, or citizen can just ask to see the officers' video tapes at the end of the day. That way, they can experience everything almost first-hand without actually risking life and limb.

A ride-a-long would be on my F**k-It List.

GO ON THE FASTEST, SCARIEST, ROLLER COASTER

I'm betting that when some sort of theme park, be it Disneyland or what have you, decide to put in the world's scariest roller coaster, and put the job up for public tender, are not likely to go with the highest bidder.

Rather, they will go with the lowest bidder. The low bidder has found some way to build this roller coaster cheaper than his competitor, either by using less, or inferior material, or cutting labor costs. But, somewhere along the line, he is going to be cutting corners.

This is what I think of when I go on some ride or form of transport, be it a roller coaster or an airplane. I am climbing into or onto a mode of transport that was built by the lowest bidder.

Now, once this company gets the contract, and finds out what all the other bids were, and how much money they left sitting on the table, they probably would not be a happy campers, and, this could reflect in the way they built their roller coaster.

With that in mind, I have some trepidation about going on these modes of transport, as I feel the person who built this, might have the same attitude that I would; "I'll get back at those bastards for making me put in such a low bid."

Thus, I will create a few; 'flaws', or; 'overlooks'. Not enough to not hurt nor kill anyone, but enough to make sure, I'll be called back to rectify the problem, at an additional cost, of course.

So, assuming the person who contracted to build this roller coaster is a like-minded thinker, I would not only be quite reluctant, but downright adamant, to the prospect of riding this life-threatening roller coaster.

I know there are people out there, who make it their goal in life to ride all the most dangerous and scariest roller coasters, but, I am not one of them. Sure, very few get killed, but, the few who do, only get killed once. That's how it works.

On my F**k-It List goes riding on the world's fastest and scariest roller coaster.

TRY TIGHT-ROPE WALKING

As to date, I have never been to Niagara
Falls. Neither, prior to their destruction, was
I at the World Trade Centers. Either way,
had I ever been at one of those locations, I
can absolutely gauranfriggintee you, I would
not want to walk across the Falls, nor from
tower One to tower Two, on a piece of wire.

I'm just not in that big of a hurry. If I am at
either place and want to get to the other side,
I'll go on the ground and walk across.

I've seen videos of these fearless, high-wire
characters walking between two fixed
structures, high above the ground or the
water, using just a simple pole to balance
them, all the while walking on a wire rope.

Needless to say, watching them from the
safety and confines of my living room still
gave me the, 'willies'.

What could possibly make a person try such
a feat is beyond my comprehension. True,
they can hold some kind of a record, but,
once they have grown too old, sick, weak or
feeble to do this anymore, will that record

really hold any water when they're filling
out a resume for a new job? I seriously
doubt it.

After all, how many jobs are there out there,
that require a person to walk, from one place
to another, on a wire high above the ground?
I can't, off the top of my head, think of a
single one, save bridge building.

Granted, there aren't many of these people
out there, and for good reason. Only a
minute amount of people in this world want
to risk their lives for a fleeting moment of
glory.

I've walked across the top of a fence when I
was a younger lad, and as I recall, fell half a
dozen times before I reached the end.
Fortunately I was only three feet off the
ground, thus sustained no injuries, other than
taunts from my mates.

If I had a bucket list, which I don't, this
particular venture would not be on it.
Rather, it will be going on my F**k-It. List.

GO BACKPACKING

People like to, 'get back to nature', even though they were never there in the first place, and grew up entirely in a large metropolis, with the only large uninhabited land mass they see, being an urban park.

However, it seems more and more people are into, 'adventure' getaways, and holidays. Backpacking up into the mountains for a few days seems to attract a lot of people.

They want to become 'one', with the flora and fauna in the wild. They want to experience what it might be like to set foot upon a piece of land, where possibly no man has ever set foot upon before.

This could be done on the prairies. A person could go out onto a field or pasture, where possibly no man had ever set foot. However, there is no risk of life, or adventure here. Especially when you can drive right up to the sight you want to explore, in your camper.

This is why people choose to go hiking up remote and dangerous mountains, where they know they will not likely encounter other human beings, and, that is exactly what they're after.

Of course, they have no idea what they are getting themselves into. They have never experienced poison oak or poison ivy. Wouldn't know if they saw it, and if they came in contact with it, wouldn't know what to do about it.

They have never seen bears, cougars, moose and an array of other wild and ferocious beasts in the wilds. They all look cute on some nature show. Look like you could walk up to them and pet them. Not so.

With backpacking, you're carrying all your supplies on your back, including your little house, commonly referred to as a tent. This tent gives you about as much protection against wild animals and the elements as if you were to cover yourself with toilet paper.

Up in the mountains there are steep drop-offs, crevices, loose and falling rock. This is how Mother Nature made things. Why challenge Mother Nature? On my F**k-It List., is where backpacking belongs.

GO ZIP LINING

This is an alternative, albeit, not a real great one, to going up on a high place such as a tower, and jumping off. With this sport, if you can call it that. you don't really jump off, vis a vis letting loose of a support.

No. You jump off a tower that is attached to some structure by a cable at a far lower level than the tower you're jumping off, then, travel at breakneck-speed while sitting in a harness of some sort, or hanging on to a wheel with handles.

In the first place, before you even get to your jump-off tower, you have to hike up to it, and, that can be a daunting task. So once you get to the top, you'd better be sure you have the courage to jump off, and take the fast way down, otherwise you have a long walk down again, although not quite so arduous as the walk up.

At the tower, there'll be some kid, who does this as an after-school, or summer job, and he will tell you have nothing to worry about. All the while, forcing you to the edge of the platform from where you are going to depart, whether you want to or not.

The contraption you are going to be strapped into, or hanging from, basically is just made up of a single or more wheels. And we all know how fast wheels can turn especially when they have some weight on them, and the angle of descent is at least forty-five degrees.

I'm guessing once a person leaves the top platform, and picks up speed, that could be somewhat unsettling. At the end, to slow down the descent, the cable takes a turn upwards, and there might me another part-time kid there to catch you, as it were.

I can see a fifty pound person stopping with some ease, but how about a two-hundred and fifty pound person? Not going to stop so quick, I'd be guessing.

I'm not what you'd call obese, but I'm sure, if I was hurtling toward a point on a wire holding on to a wheel, I could probably go right through the great Wall of China. Not a risk I need to take. On my F**k-It List, goes this adventure.

JOIN THE ALASKA IDITAROD

The Iditarod Trail Dog Sled Race, is an
annual long-distance race run in early March
from Anchorage to Nome, Alaska.

It encompasses a trek of over five-hundred
miles, and can take from nine to fifteen
days, depending on weather conditions.

Needles to say, in that neck of the woods,
and, at that time of year, you won't be
basking in the sun's warmth.

This is not a sport for the faint-of-heart, so,
that automatically leaves me out. Teams
race through blizzards, and winds that can
bring the chill factor to one-hundred degrees
below zero.

The trail is through harsh landscape; sparse
forest, along the Bering Sea shore, over hills
and mountains, and across rivers.

A, 'Musher', (person who drives the sled and
dog team) must have a team of sixteen dogs.
I'm guessing these dogs get real hungry
doing all that work, and, I wouldn't want to
fall down in front of them.

66

First off, there are several words just in the title of this event that would deter me; dog; sled; racing; Alaska.

All these tell me that I will be trusting my fate to animals, I'll be travelling in an open conveyance, I'll be going fast, and, I'll be way up north, in the cold.

I can't begin to comprehend what would induce people to participate in such an event. The last thing I want in life, is to freeze my ass off before the rest of me freezes. That's just a plain, nasty way to die.

I could get attacked by wolves, bears, or even my own dogs, but the part that scares me rather than being eaten alive is; freezing to death.

I could maybe see myself partaking in a dog race on the beaches of southern California, but, up in Alaska, forget about it.

On my F**k-It List goes the Iditarod.

COMPETE IN THE TOUGH- GUY COMPETITION

This is a competition that was started in 1987 in England. The title is self-explanatory. This is considered the toughest competition in the world, with one-third of the entrants failing to make it to the finish.

Being as how I am not close to any of the participants, neither figuratively nor literally, I can call them a special kind of stupid.

Naturally, if I ever come face-to-face with any of these dudes, I'll be showering praise and admiration upon them like there's no tomorrow.

Apparently there is a winter and summer version of this competition, with the winter one being the most challenging.

Participants must go through some twenty-five grueling obstacles during this seven or eight mile run. Up and down hills, freezing pools, fire pits, barbed wire, electric shocks, and the list goes on.

Before taking part in this event, participants must sign what they call a; 'death warrant'. This absolves the organizers of any liability.

Right there, that paper in itself would cause me concern. If I choose to go on a roller coaster, or in the Boston Marathon, I don't have to sign such a document. This tells me, that what I'm about to partake in, is a risk to my life. Therefore, I am not real keen on it.

What is the end result here? So you're a winner, and considered a 'tough guy'. How does that enhance your life? Will you get a better seat on a bus, train or plane? Will you be given a special place in a restaurant? I doubt it, unless you beat up the maitre d'.

What's to say, you won't come out of the competition the winner, and on your way to your car, get run over by one of the losers, as he is so distraught at losing.

The only way I'd enter such this competition would be if; I was competing against old, invalid people. Then, I'd kick ass, Other than that, on my F**k-It List goes; the Tough Guy Competition.

TRAVEL TO NORTH OR SOUTH POLES

This has been done to death. Years ago, the first person, although this is disputed, to reach the North Pole was Frederick Cook, in 1908. Purportedly, the first person to reach the south Pole, was Roald Amundsen.

Since these times, there have been literally hundreds of people, who have made it a life's goal to trek to either of these poles.

Too bad some guy from Poland wasn't the first to discover either, or both poles. That way they could say that a Pole was the first to a pole. Just a little humor I'd thought I'd throw in there.

At any rate, there are still people every year, who want to retrace either of these early explorers, and get to one pole or the other.

As you can well imagine, this is not an easy feat, as both poles are distant, cold, and remote. Getting to them by land requires weeks of trekking over solid ice, and camping out in the barren wasteland.

Is my hat off to such hardy adventurers? Not hardly. To me it's a good thing that being stupid isn't against international law, or all these people would be biding their time in a prison somewhere. Maybe in the North or South Poles, if they have prisons there.

As far as I'm concerned, once something has been discovered, leave it at that, and move on. You're not gaining anything by being the second , third or tenth person to that site. Who cares? Not me. That's who not.

People seem to have no problem with putting their life, and other's lives in peril, to accomplish some sort of moot goal.

I suppose they want their fifteen minutes of fame, and, trust me, that's about all they'll get. No one cares what they did. For one day, it might make the headline on the upper fold, but, after that, people move on to more pressing things in their lives.

Do I want to make either trek and risk freezing my ass off, to an invisible pole? Not. Here's another item on my F**k-It List.

ATTEMPT FIREWALKING

Apparently, as I've been told, people who are in the, 'motivation' business recommend this to their clients, as a means of getting focused.

Yeah. this is what I call getting focused; walking barefoot across a pit of hot, burning coals.

I can't help but wonder, who the first person was to try this, and what his mindset was. Perhaps he was trying to impress some babe, as this would be the only reason I would do it.

The firewalker guy says to her; " Babe. See that pit over there filled with red-hot coals. Watch this."

I've seen videos of people, and not jungle people that you might expect, but white, business people, running across these fire pits. When I say running, I mean running. Hot-footing is more like it, as I feel that pun will fit real nice here.

Naturally, first-off they have some trepidation, until some 'seasoned' person, or guide does it first. Then, with a crowd of drunken workmates cheering him or her on, that person, being several sheets to the wind themselves, will dash like a mad fool across the hot coals.

Once safely across, they will say it wasn't such a big deal, and coax the next poor drunken sucker to follow suit.

I recall in my younger years, being on a beach, and barefoot. I accidentally stepped on someone's discarded cigarette butt. Let me tell you, I didn't have to step on more than just that one, to convince me never to do it again. I couldn't even see myself running over a pit of burning cigarette butts, let alone a pit of hot coals.

Truth be told, I can't even see me running over a pit of hot coals with my shoes on. I can only guess how quick rubber sneakers melt, and the last thing I want to pull off my feet is melted rubber.

On my F**k-It List goes this firewalking thing.

GO CAVING

There are not a lot of people into this, 'sport', as opposed to other adventurous sports. However, their number seems to be growing.

What, 'caving' entails; is to find out-of-the way caves, (which caves aren't out of the way?) with possibly no end to their vertical or horizontal depths, and explore them.

For this, the, 'caver', will need a few associates, torches or flashlights, and lots of rope.

This can be a very perilous undertaking, as, if you are one of the first, or, in fact *the* very first person to explore a cave, you have no idea as to what awaits you.

You could drop into an bottomless pit, and no one could ever recover your body. You could encounter a cave-in, as you may be disturbing rocks that have sat in a precarious manner for many, perhaps hundreds, of years, and your slightest movement can cause them to come tumbling down.

Before you even attempt such an undertaking, make absolutely sure you are not claustrophobic, for, if you are, you are beat before you start.

I suppose there is something to be said for people who want to discover new things. For, if there weren't such people we would never have, nor know about, new things.

I have no problem with other people risking their lives to possibly benefit me somewhere down the road. But, I'll be damned if I 'd do the same for anyone else.

I am somewhat claustrophobic, don't like dark or deep places. Don't like the idea of putting my life in the hands of a piece of rope, or some other fellow caver.

If I want to go into some kind of cave, I'll go to Disneyland. they have lots of them there. and, that way, if I don't get out safely, I'll be able to sue them. That scenario appeals to me.

On my F**k-It List goes caving.

DO FREEHAND ROCK CLIMBING

This is a sport whereby you climb up high rocks as in Utah, without a safety rope. Perhaps the reader has not picked up on it yet, so, I'll just come right out with it; I do not like risking my life for any reason.

There are enough things I have to worry about on a daily basis to keep me out of harm's way. I don't need to go out of my way to create any, or, 'push the envelope', as they say.

No doubt about it, these rock climbers, the ones who scale shear rocks without benefit of ropes, are fearless individuals.

However, most people are born with a certain amount of fear of one thing or another. and, I think that's a good thing.

If no one had any fear of anything, imagine what the world would be like. You'd have all sorts of people on the highways and freeways driving two-hundred miles per hour.

You'd have people swimming across rivers instead of taking the bridge. You'd have people in zoos, all over the world jumping in the lions' cages.

If no one had fear, then who would entertain us, and make us pay attention to fearless feats? Fear is something almost everyone has, and, I have it in spades.

I like being fearful, that way, I know I won't have to risk my life. If I were in a war and my commander told me to jump out of my foxhole and charge the enemy, I'd say, "I don't think so, I fear the enemy." Then he'd just pick the next guy, who had no fear, and, likely as not, that guy would get killed or maimed, and I'd be just fine. That works for me. Fear, has its advantages.

I don't need to take up rock climbing, as I know that there is nothing at the top, except the top of the rock, and, I've seen rock tops before, they aren't all that impressive. Even if I did get into rock climbing, a rope, a parachute, and a safety net would be high on my list of, 'must have' items. Failing that, rock climbing goes on my F**k-It List.

GET A TATTOO OR EARRING

Although neither of these, like so many
other things, are dangerous, per se. I have no
desire for either.

In my day, only women had earrings, and
only sailors had tattoos. Nowadays,
everyone has both. The thing that gets me
here is; it's the women who have the tattoos,
and the men who have the earrings.

You'll also see a lot of women with what I'd
call, 'butch' haircuts, while men, and some
of them big, mean-looking bruisers, sporting
pony tails.

What the hell is going on in this world? Was
there some time-line that I wasn't informed
about whereby the sexes had to switch
roles?

As far as a tattoo, I could tolerate it if a
person, meaning a man, had one on his
forearm. Or, even if a woman had a tiny rose
tattoo or her ankle, maybe even on her ass,
although chances of me seeing the latter are
slim to none. But, that's okay.

Seeing people with tattoos from head to foot, to me, is just as bad as seeing someone with elephantiasis. At least with the latter, it was something that the person who had it, did not have on purpose.

Earrings. These belong on women, but, only on their ears, thus the name. Earrings do not belong on tongues, lips, cheeks, belly buttons or any other such body protrusion, part, or appendage.

For some reason, beyond my comprehension, getting a tattoo or getting several, and, getting an earring or several, is a goal of many people today, mostly younger, but not limited to them.

I personally do not have any buds who have tattoos or earrings, if they did, they would cease to be my buds. I do not hang with any tattooed nor earringed people, as, I don't like attention drawn towards me.

High on my F**k-It List, goes the desire to have either a tattoo or an earring, either on my ass or ear, as the case may be, unless I plan on getting a job as a circus side-show geek.

79

RUN THE BOSTON MARATHON

Every year, in Boston, Massachusetts, they have their world-famous Marathon. A competition, in which runners world-wide partake.

This marathon attracts approximately thirty-thousand participants, and the total length of the marathon is over twenty-six miles.

Now, you may be asking yourself, as I did, who has so much time on their hands, that they will plan, and train for this for months, even years? I don't have that answer, as yet.

I have no problem driving twenty-six miles, and if I have to race someone in the process, so be it. But, the end result will be, that once I cross the finish line, I will not be all hot and sweaty, nor on the verge of having a heart attack.

Prior to 1986, the only prize for winning this marathon was a wreath woven from olive branches. Big friggin' whoop.

Then, along came professional runners, and they would not run unless they were financially compensated. So much for professionalism. At any rate, the first prize is now a whopping one-hundred and fifty grand.

I have to come clean here, and admit that at one time I had considered entering this race. However, they have all sorts of silly rules like; if someone is passing you, you cannot trip them, or you would be disqualified. is this a race for adults or wimps?

At any rate, I have no intention of risking going into cardiac arrest, just for the sake of being faster than someone else in a foot-race. No one, except the second and third-place finishers, ever remembers who the winner was anyway.

I'm not going to get all sweaty, dress like some damn fool in a halter top and shorts possibly sporting a bandanna, just for a lousy one-hundred and fifty grand. I can make more robbing a bank. No sweat.

The Boston Marathon runs on to my F**k-It List.

HUNT WILD BOAR

They are not called 'wild' boar because they're tame and friendly. They are wild in every sense of the word; they live in the wild, and they act wild.

Hunting and killing them is not the cakewalk one would perceive it to be. Wild boars are fast, cunning, and will not hesitate to charge a person. They are not unlike a pit-bull. The madder you make it, and the more wounded it is, the more it will come after you seeking revenge.

I like pork: Bacon, pork chops, ribs, pork roast, you name it, if there's a pork meal, I'm there. However, I refuse to risk my life for it. That's where I draw the line.

Mind you, I have been to supermarkets when there was a sale on such an item as say; Kraft Dinner, and became embroiled in a fisticuff confrontation, on more than one occasion with some womenfolk, who felt they needed the product to feed their kids, more than I needed it to feed my KD addiction. But, that's another story.

This, so called 'sport' has been around in various U.S. places for many years, but is just now becoming popular in western Canada. Where the wild boars came from, is anybody's guess, but they're here.

Wild boars are somewhat nocturnal. So, a lot of the hunts go on during the night. Meaning, when it's dark, and you can't see the boar, but, it can see you. Generally, a person will go in some form of all-terrain vehicle, oftentimes have dogs, and go through dense bush looking for these boar.

Sometimes, the boar is hiding in the bush where it can see you, and waits until you get close enough, so it can charge out, and shred you to ribbons with its razor-sharp tusks.

The way I see it; live, and let live. The boar did nothing to me, so I won't do anything to it. My hunger for pork, has yet to overcome my fear, of a pork. It's much easier and safer to go to my local supermarket and just pick up a package when I need it. If customers or the butcher are a little wild, that, I can tolerate. If I'm going to hunt any animal, it will be sheep, but, as for hunting wild boar, that goes on my F**k-It List.

BE A MENTOR

There are people out there, who would like
to be a mentor to someone in some fashion.
These, 'mentor' types are, likely as not,
compassionate, caring people. Right there,
that rules me out.

A mentor first off, has to have some talent or
knowledge that he or she can pass along. I
have talents I could pass along, but, I doubt
if too many people, especially youngsters,
want, or need to know, how to smoke, drink
beer and cuss. Although the former is
becoming more of a rarity.

At any rate, being a mentor requires time
and patience, neither of which I have, or, if I
do, am not willing to waste it on some kid
who I don't know, nor care about.

People take great pride in being a mentor,
especially if after the process is completed,
and the results are good, they can claim they
helped so and so on his or her journey
through life.

The way I look at it, there are schools,
vocational and conventional, universities,

colleges, and apprenticeship programs, all of which are supposed to educate and inform the uneducated and uninformed.

So, what is the real need for the average Joe or Jane to take time out of their lives to teach individuals, when there are already intuitions in place strictly for that purpose?

Perhaps, when all is said and done, it's a vanity thing. A mentor can claim bragging rights for helping little Johnny or little Susie.

Then again, as would be the case with me, it could be a I.O.U. thing. With this, if I helped someone out in life, I would expect something back in return. Perhaps I set them on a path whereby they would become wealthy or famous. No question about it, I'd want to cash in on either of those, or both.

However, the chances of me mentoring someone are about as good as me getting the Nobel Prize for compassion. Don't think that's happening anytime soon. So, mentoring, goes on my F**k-It List it.

CARRY THE OLYMPIC TORCH

This is something former, present or future athletes covet. My athletic abilities and interests start and end with beer-drinking and cigar smoking, and I'm quite proficient at both. However, since there is not an event in the Olympics for either of those talents, I have no interest in running through the streets with fire on a stick, any more than I have in running with scissors.

People will literally carry this Olympic torch across an entire country. Why? Why not just buy a Bic lighter at the end of the course where the Olympics are going to be held, and light the damn torch there? That's probably what I would do.

Neither running, nor running with fire, have ever been what I'd call a top priority in my life. I can quite easily go through my life having done neither, and have no regrets.

Crowds, that's another thing I should perhaps mention, that I don't like. Even, if I'd want to run through streets carrying a fire- stick, I would be quite hesitant about anyone witnessing it.

86

When you see these torch-carrying folk, running through the streets, you'll also see those streets lined with people cheering them on.

Why is this necessary? It's not like the torch carriers are in the actual Olympics, and will be getting some medal at the end. No. They're just possible losers who couldn't make it into the Olympics, carrying the torch to the site, where the real athletes will be participating.

Is it possible that some ordinary Joe carrying the Olympic torch, can run faster than some of the Olympians? Perhaps there should be an Olympic event for Olympic torch carrying.

Just out of spite, because that's the kind of person I am, if I was at the Olympic site, and present when the last torch bearer, brought the flame, just before he lit the eternal torch at the site, I'd walk up with a fire extinguisher, and put it out. Then, they'd have to go back to the other end of the country, and start all over. Carrying the Olympic torch is a hot item on my F**k-It List.

GO ON AN AFRICAN SAFARI

This is high on a lot of people's bucket list. For some reason, which escapes me at this time, they feel that if they get into the wilds of Africa, they'll be one with nature.

These safaris entail riding in an air-conditioned vehicle, having a cooler full of beer, wine, and sandwiches. Just where is the real adventure here?

You can see wild animals on any continent, you don't have to go to Africa. In Canada and the United states, go out in the country and there are all sorts of racoons, gophers, rabbits and the like. What more do you want? At least with these animals there is minimal risk to your life.

In many cases here in North America, you don't even have to go into the wild to see wild animals, they'll come to you. How many times have you seen home photos of bears and cougars coming into someone's yard in a city?

I've seen videos, as I'm sure everyone has, where people go into the wilds of Africa, and are literally attacked by some wild and atrocious animal: a tiger, a lion, and irate elephant. These animals are on their turf. They don't want you there taking photos and 'oohing', and 'aaahing', while they're resting, eating or chasing down their next meal. They think that's stupid, and quite frankly, so do I.

There are two types of African safaris; one for tourists, to see animals in the wild, and one for hunters to kill animals in the wild. I'm guessing of the two, the wild animals would dislike the hunting and killing safaris the most. Unfortunately the animals can't tell the tourists from the hunters, until it's too late, and the guns come out.

I am not into killing animals, and, even if I was, I wouldn't travel thousands of miles and spend thousands of dollars to do it. That also applies to gawking at them.

African safaris are for killers or tourists. I'm neither. Therefore, an African Safari goes on my F**k-It List.

BUILD HOUSES IN THIRD-WORLD COUNTRIES FOR HABITAT FOR HUMANITY

This is a great organization. They do a lot of good works, and, I'm for organizations that do good for others less fortunate. I just don't want to be an active participant.

I'm not saying I'm totally averse to doing such a thing, just not in a Third-World country.

Here in Canada, we have the Habitat for Humanity organization in most cities. Although I have never worked on a project, and don't see that happening in the near future. I possibly could. Probably won't, but, I could.

Working up here, building houses, at least, affords me certain luxuries, I would not otherwise have in a poor Third-World country.

In a Third-World country, likely as not I'd be out in the middle of nowhere, living in some temporary abode, such as a tent without running water or electricity.

90

This is not acceptable to me. I have no problem making a sacrifice to help others, providing that sacrifice does not inconvenience me to any great, or, lesser, degree. Compassion only goes so far in my book.

If I provide my labor free, the least the Habitat organization could do is put me up in a five-star with everything comped. After all, at the end of a hard day of ordering foreign peasants around, a man would get powerful tired and need to unwind.

There are lots of people who continuously go to poor countries and build houses for the less fortunate. Good on them, and, it is for that reason, I don't feel I have to.

I don't understand why Habitat doesn't just put all the homeless people up in mobile homes, and that way no one would have to volunteer their time.

I believe building homes for the Habitat for Humanity in a Third World country, will go right there on my F**k-It List.

FIND JESUS

Seems to me, there are a lot of people out there trying to find Jesus. Probably the same amount, who claim to already have found Him. Maybe the people who found Him should tell the people looking for Him, where to look.

I've heard it said that if a person truly wants to disappear, he or she can do so, with some thought, planning and ingenuity.

This is for the common man or woman. I imagine, it is easier for Jesus to disappear. This is a guy who can turn water into wine, for crying out loud. He can heal lepers, and do all sorts of cool tricks. With all His abilities, I'd venture to guess that hiding would be a cake-walk for Him.

Why Jesus would want to hide is anyone's guess. My guess would be that He is just tired of all the notoriety He's achieved over the last few hundred years, and wants some, 'alone' time.

No doubt, once people back in the biblical days, saw just what Jesus could do, everyone and his dog, put the arm on Him to perform some miracle, to enhance their lives.

In this day and age, you'd have people wanting Him to give them the numbers of the next Powerball lottery. Or, reveal which next new tech company, was going to go on to be worth billions in a few short months. The favors people would ask of Him would be endless.

Therefore, it's my opinion that the aforementioned is the reason Jesus cannot be found, and, does not want to be found.

People spend all their lives trying to find Jesus. and, those who claim to have found Him already, well, I'm somewhat skeptic about their claims, as no one has ever produced Jesus in the flesh, nor have any photos, or, selfies of Him with them.

Jesus doesn't want me, nor anyone else to find Him, so, I'll let Him be, and put trying to find Him, on my F**k-It List.

ATTEND AN OPERA

I have no problem with a fat lady singing,
but, if that lady has a robe with a fur collar
and a hat with horns on it, I'm sorry, that's
just not my thing. These events are attended
by, 'high society, of which I'm not.

Operas are traditional among German and
Italian aristocracy. As such, they are, likely
as not, sung in either German or Italian. This
I can understand, if a person is attending a
opera in Germany or Italy respectively.

So, I'm wondering when operas are
performed here in North America, why are
they still done in either the German or
Italian language?

Surely there aren't that many people who
can understand either language ,who are of
the opera crowd.

There's no question that the singers, be they
men or women, have a good set of pipes, as
one can hear them all over the opera hall,
sans the benefit of a public address system.

I have no problem going to some kind of a musical like 'West Side Story', whereby I can understand the lyrics and, which, as a rule, has a 'modern day' theme. But, damned if I'm going to sit though a musical whereby I can neither understand the language, and, consequently not understand what the people on stage are trying to convey.

If I went to an opera, for whatever reason, I can't fathom, likely as not, I'd have some sort of Walkman, or i-phone. So while the fat lady, and all her companions on stage were singing about this or that, I could be listening to a good Willie Nelson song.

I've no doubt that all the, 'high brows;' who attend operas, have no more of a clue than I do, about what they're singing about, or what the whole damn opera is about. They go to operas, because that's what rich people do.

Attending an opera is way high up on my F**k-It List, whether the opera is in German, Italian or even, in English. Screw the fat lady with her horns.

VOLUNTEER AT A SOUP KITCHEN

A lot of people do this sort of thing,
especially round-about Christmas time.

These same volunteers, will pass street
people every day of the week, and not give
them a second thought, let alone offer to
serve or cook them a meal.

Along comes Christmas, and everyone is
front-and-center, to volunteer to work in a
soup kitchen.

These volunteers maintain they are,
'sacrificing' their time, away from their
families, to be with the less fortunate.
Really? That's why they're doing this?

Do they think the street people only need to
be served a meal once a year, at Christmas?
Were that the case, the homeless would be
looking pretty gaunt come Christmas, and,
no doubt, quite famished.

Where are these people, these volunteers,
the rest of the year?

I'll probably never volunteer to work in a soup kitchen at Christmas, Easter, or any other time of the year. Why? I am not a, waiter, a cook, nor a volunteer.

In the first place, I think it's enough that some shelters cook and prepare the meal for these people. Why do they have to serve it as well? Haven't these street people ever been to a buffet?

They have lots of time. They can walk through a line and pick out what they want, or don't want to eat, without being catered to. I do it. Why can't they? That's how I feel.

If a soup kitchen was in fact, exactly that; a soup kitchen, maybe I could get involved. Dump a ladle of soup in their bowl, they eat it, and they're out back on the street.

However, a 'soup' kitchen is so much more these days; they will serve sandwiches, and full-course meals. I call that a restaurant, and, I do not work in restaurants.

Volunteering at a soup kitchen will be another item on my F**k-It List.

LEARN A NEW LANGUAGE

Population wise, the English language, per se, is spoken by far less people on the planet than languages such as Chinese, Arabic or African languages.

However, English is the most commonly accepted language around the world. If you want to be on the world language band-wagon, you'd better know how to speak English, or, you're going to be left in the dust.

We Anglos, can't be bothered with learning some foreign language. However, we fully expect foreigners to learn our language. We're funny that way. Not, ha ha funny but, arrogant funny. Sorry, foreign, non-English speaking folks, but, that's just the way we are.

No doubt, it can't hurt learning another language. Perhaps I'm stranded up on Mount Everest, and I want to radio a Sherpa to risk his life and come up to save me. That would be a time, I'd want to know the Sherpa language.

Should I take a trip to Germany without my wife, and, end up in a tavern with some foxy looking Frauleins, that would be a time I'd like to know German. However, both former scenarios are remote, at best.

Naturally, if I were to move to some foreign country, it would serve me well to know their language. However, the way I see it, if they want to communicate with me, they should learn mine.

I'm guessing that learning a new language is not all that easy, not to mention time-consuming. Some languages, such as, Chinese, simply baffle me. How do the Chinese do it? To me, they'd be better off learning sign language.

It would be just my luck that I'd pick a language such as Spanish to learn, then wind up with my life in peril in France, and not being able to communicate with anyone.

I'm guessing no time soon, maybe even, never. Okay. Never, am I going to learn a foreign language, so, on my F**k-It List that goes.

TREK TO TIBET TO GET ENLIGHTENED

The Dalai Lama is the spiritual leader of the Tibetan people, and is a man respected by secular and non secular people around the world. (He reminds me a lot of myself. Not the leader/respected part, but, neither of us are tall, and, we both wear glasses.)

I believe, but am not one-hundred percent sure, he is the brother, or some kin, to Tony Lama, the famous western boot maker.

At any rate, although he lives in exile in India, his roots are in Tibet. Thus, many people consider Tibet a spiritual place to visit, to gain enlightenment, and to meditate.

They will make it a life's goal to trek to Tibet, to perhaps discover the meaning of life.

Personally, I'm not convinced life really has any meaning, if you know what I mean. Life is life. You go through it, have your ups and downs, then you die. What's the big mystery? God put us on this planet just so we'd end up dead. End of story.

I've never been to Tibet, and, don't plan to go there in the near future, or, even the far future. Tibet is the highest region on earth, and can boast being the home of Mount Everest. Perhaps because of its altitude, that makes it a special place to meditate, as the air is a lot lighter. I don't know.

I'm guessing that getting to Tibet, is no walk in the park, as no matter where you come from, it will be all uphill. One probably has to endure all sorts of deprivations, as I'm sure being at that height in that country, will have a big-time lack of amenities.

I don't know if Tibetans themselves do a lot of praying and meditating, or, if that's just a tourist thing.

If they do, apparently the praying isn't working out too well for them, as all they seem to possess , clothing-wise, are; robes and sandals. Maybe they meditate about their lack of material trappings. and sandals. What's the whole point of life without material things?

I can meditate quite nicely in my den. A Tibetan trek is high on my F**k-It List.

EXPLORE AN ACTIVE VOLCANO

Volcanists, at they're referred to, are people
who study active volcanoes.

They will hike up a mountain, sometimes
one that is spewing out hot ash and lava,
take some tests, samples and temperatures,
so the rest of the world will know just how
hot molten rock is.

I've never put my hand in, nor stepped in,
molten rock, nor do I have to, as I already
know from its glow, that's it's damn hot.

Aside from these volcano scientists, there
are a number of people who go to active
volcanoes just to say they've done it, or, to
see for themselves what an active volcano is
like.

Risking life and limb to get a first-hand
experience at something, is not high on my
'must-do' list. As a matter of fact, it isn't
even on my 'must do' list, and even lacks
exposure on my; 'maybe-will do' list.

There are lots of things I'd like to see, in this
world, but, molten rock is not one of them.

102

I'm guessing that once a person reaches the edge of the crater atop a mountain with an active volcano, all they can expect to see is a big, round swimming pool-like hole, filled with molten rock.

Hardly a surprise there. I don't know what else they were expecting to see, but, in any case, that is all they are going to see.

Let's assume that at the same time these curious monkeys are standing on the edge of the crater, the mountain erupts. What are their chances of getting away safely? First off, the only way they have to go, is down, and that's exactly the direction in which the molten rock will flow. It's a gravity thing.

I know that the molten rock doesn't fall as fast as water, but, it doesn't have to, it can take its time. The dummy on the other hand, has to be in high-boot to outrun it. That's if the mountain didn't spew out any ash, and comer him and possibly suffocate him first.

Instead of doing this, I'll tune into YouTube, and watch some other character filming volcanoes and risking his life. It works real fine for me. On my F**k-It List this goes.

BE KIND TO A STRANGER

First off, as a youngster, I was told never to talk to strangers. Now, should I encounter a stranger who is in need, perhaps hanging by his or her fingers on the edge of a cliff, screaming for help, I may, or, may not, indulge them in a conversation pertaining to their circumstance, as, they're a stranger.

There is a reason that strangers are called 'strangers'; that is because we don't know them, and, perhaps it should stay that way, as that works out quite well for me.

That said, if my life was in peril, or I otherwise needed some assistance or advice from a stranger, I would hope they were of the Christian kind, and give me assistance. Even though I might not do the same for them, they should set a good example.

Being kind to anyone, let alone a stranger. is something a person, especially myself, has to give a lot of thought to. Kindness does not come without risks, any more than hatred does. A person doesn't go around hating everyone on the planet, nor should they go around being kind to everyone on the planet.

Kindness is not just a platitude you conger up at will, but rather, should be in your character make-up. As it turns out, that is not conducive to my particular character make-up.

Being kind to a stranger is not unlike being kind to a stray dog. You may pet and nurture this stray dog, however, at any moment, it may turn on you and bite you. In which case you, as I would, will probably immediately get your gun out, and, put it down.

Strangers are the same. You can be kind and loving to them, as I could be, but they could turn around and attack you, in which case, as with a dog, you'd want to beat them or, put them down. Unfortunately, unlike with a dog, you can't do that to people. Apparently, it's against the law, in most countries.

I feel that perhaps, only strangers should help out, and be kind, to other strangers. Should some stranger in need approach me for one thing or another, I would feel more comfortable by pointing him to another stranger and asking that person. Therefore, I'm putting kindness to strangers on my F**k-It List.

GET MYSELF A PONY

If you did not want a pony when you were a young person, you either lived on a houseboat, or, were scared of equines. Wanting a pony, was every young kid's dream. Especially for boys.

Sure, it was okay to look under some girl's dress in school, while playing some game, or, cop an accidental feel. But pony desire far outweighed girl desire.

If I had gotten a pony when I was going to school, I would have ridden it every single day to school. Granted, it would have been a short ride, as I lived right across the street from the school, but, I'd have ridden it none the less.

Having a pony would've made me look special, and feel special. Everybody in my class would have wanted to be my best friend. I could have gotten people to bring me candy and cigarettes every day. I could have had them doing my homework, and lying for me to my teachers and parents. A pony would have made life so much simpler.

Had I had a classmate, who had a pony, I can pretty much guarantee you, that by the end of the school year, I would have had myself a new pony, and that smart-alec kid would have had a fatal accident, come Field Day.

Although I am well past my prime in life, certainly past my youth, I realize that at this stage in my life, getting a pony is somewhat moot.

Unfortunately, I made that male transition, whereby women are now more appealing to me than a pony, but, not by much.

And, even if I should still get one, as I could now, chances are if I rode it, my feet would be dragging on the ground, and the poor little equine would probably collapse under my massive weight.

However, that alone is not the primary deterrent. There are those, in some quarters, who would consider my getting a pony as somewhat infantile, and, they would not be altogether wrong. Therefore, getting a pony at my age is something that I reluctantly will be putting on my F**k-It List.

VOLUNTEER TO WORK IN A
LEPER COLONY

If I was told I was going to have, or had to have, some sort of disease, but, I could pick the one I wanted, from a list. I'd have to do some serious studying on that.

I'd certainly want to pick a disease that caused me the least amount of pain and discomfort, and, hopefully, one that had a short life span, and would be easily curable.

I'm quite confident, however, that Leprosy would more than likely be dead-last on that list. Being as how it is, hands down, one of the most grotesque of diseases. Parts of your body, mainly your digits, will literally fall off.

Aside from being extremely gross, that could be downright embarrassing. Can you imagine handing someone an object, and one, or several of your fingers remained attached to that object. Likely as not, that would be the last time that person would be travelling in your social circles, or, anyone else for that matter, once word got around.

There are people, mainly religious or medical people, who will volunteer their time to go work in a Leper colony. Good on them. The world needs more people like them, providing, I am not one of them.

I certainly have compassion for the less fortunate, and people who are suffering, or just need a helping hand.

For example, it is next to impossible to apply suntan lotion to the back of your own body. So, should I come across some babe lying on a beach and needing a suntan lotion applier, I'd be all over that. Figuratively and literally.

People would see this and say to each other; "Man, is that guy full of compassion, or what?". Damn straight. I am full of it.

However, working with lepers is not quite the same thing. If I were on the island of Molokai, and saw a babe on the beach needing a suntan lotion application, I'd probably pass worrying that one of her breasts would fall off during the rub. Therefore I'll will put working with lepers on my F**k-It List.

109

TAKE A PEER-BONDING SABBATICAL

I feel bonding is something that should occur when you apply glue to two surfaces, and stick them together. People-bonding is not something that really appeals to me.

To 'bond,' in the human sense, generally entails getting to know someone quite intimately, and having some sort of relationship, understanding or life-sharing experiences. All the aforementioned, goes against my grain.

Companies periodically, like to see their employees indulge in things of this nature. The companies are forever trying to get more production out of their employees, and think that doing so with all sorts of fuzzy-feely, get-together kinds of things, rather than just give their employees a big raise, is the answer.

Likely as not, I have a low tolerance level, of my fellow employees, if in fact, I can even stand to be around them in the first place. Thus, I refer to them as, 'fellow employees', and not friends

There are basically two kinds of people I do not like to be around, or, to have around me. those are; people who I work with, and, people who I don't work with. I'm sorry, but that's just the kind of guy I am.

To go on a work sabbatical with fellow employees, is not unlike taking them with me on a vacation, and, I can't see that happening in this lifetime.

The way I see it is this; a person spends enough time at the workplace with your fellow workers and peers. So, why would you want to take some of your precious free, away-from-work, time, to spend with them as well? There's no sense to it.

When the bosses take trips together, that involves drinking, partying, hookers and golf. When employees take trips together, that involves, discussing business, and better ways to improve production for the company. I'd much prefer if all my fellow employees went on a sabbatical without me. That would truly be a sabbatical I could enjoy. A peer-bonding sabbatical, goes on my F**k-It List.

LEARN TO PLAY A GUITAR

I think just about every guy I've ever known, including myself, at one time or another, owned a guitar.

We bought these with the best of intentions; to impress the babes. We all wanted to be like Elvis, Ricky Nelson or some other rock and roll singer whom the babes swooned over.

Buying the guitar, bringing it home and taking it out of the case was easy. No talent required there at all. The next thing was to look at the little book that came with it, or that you bought, showing several standard chords, and try to get a handle on that.

It actually wasn't all that hard to learn two or three chords right away, and play them over and over again. However, to play them over and over again, day after day, after day, was another matter. And, this is just about where we all fell by the wayside.

First off, holding the strings down tight against the frets, was somewhat painful on

112

the tips of the fingers, and no one, wants to be in pain, at least, not on the finger tips.

Learning to play a guitar takes a lot of practise, as well as loads of discipline. Much like exercising. If you don't keep at it, it just won't work, and your initial goal will not be achieved.

Of course, whenever someone comes over to your house, especially some chick or a female friend from school, you make sure the guitar is strategically placed so that said chick will see it, and be immediately impressed, even without hearing a single note or chord.

This is where you can lay it on thick, and tell her you just bought the guitar, even if you've had it for years, and strum a few chords, and she will, likely as not, be duly impressed, assured that your musical talents are just at the verge of coming out.

But, as I get older, my hands are getting a touch of the arthritis, and I'm way past impressing babes. So, learning to play a guitar is going on my F**k-It List.

113

BECOME THE PRIME MINISTER
OF CANADA

When I was a youngster, as with most young people, especially boys, I told my share of lies. I did this for various reasons: get something I wanted; get out of some jam; blame a transgression I had committed on someone else. Whatever. Lying served me well back then. Still does.

Now that I have matured, to a degree, I pretty much no longer lie. Okay, the odd time for the same above reasons, but, not as much as I used to. That said, I don't know if I would be comfortable being a compulsive liar as part of, my livelihood.

I'm referring here now, to the life of a politician. It makes no difference whether that politician is on the municipal, provincial or federal level. They all seem to be cut from the same bolt of cloth. Prior to going into politics, these people seem to be of good character. However, once they're elected to office, they go through a metamorphosis, whereby honesty and integrity, take a back seat to power and prestige.

114

This holds true regarding the Prime Minister of Canada. In the entire history of Canada, there has not been one, not one, Prime Minster, who has not reneged on his, or her, promises.

What's the point of making promises if you don't keep, nor even attempt, to keep them? Once you're in, it will be at least four years until the next election, then you can make a lot more promises. The rank and file voters are so naive, they will not see your scam.

If a man running for Prime Minster of Canada, told the electorate that he would make it illegal for any politician to lie to the public, he'd be lying about that. But, he'd probably get elected, and , by then it would be too late.

The Canadian prime minister has to know how to speak French, for all those Quebec frogs. He gets little, or no respect, from any other country as Canada doesn't have any juice, militarily or otherwise. The Canadian PM is invited to world summits, just as an in-law is invited to a family gathering. No one wants to offend him. The Prime Minister's job is for sure on my F**k-It List.

SEARCH FOR THE ABOMINABLE SNOWMAN

Despite numerable supposed sightings, and even a photo or video or two, this character seems as elusive as Elvis.

Maybe he, or she, exists, I don't know. If so, for whatever reason, it does not seem to be a sociable animal.

Apparently, according to those who claim to have seen it, it runs away from people. I don't blame it, as I tend to do that as well.

Nonetheless, there are countless people who spend a lot of time, some even all their time, pursuing this elusive animal-being.

Reports I've seen and read, describe this thing as being quite tall and muscular. Also, it can belt out a hair-raising, blood-curdling roar, and has a foul odor about it. Each and every one of the aforementioned descriptions increases the likelihood of me not wanting to go looking for it.

In the first place, all indications point to this creature, wanting to be left alone, and to the degree, it could become violent if its privacy were invaded.

Being as how people have searched for this creature for decades, and never had close contact with it, I'm guessing I wouldn't fare any better.

Even if I were to go to look for this creature, and found it, meaning being in close contact. What then? Am I going to train it to follow me? Am I going to wrestle it to the ground? Not hardly. I guessing if I came close to it, that would be the last anyone heard from me.

Spending weeks, months and years, out in the woods living in a makeshift tent and eating berries just to catch some unknown creature, that was likely to kill me, is not all that appealing. Hell, I can't even catch some babe when she's jogging past my house, in plain sight. So what are my chances of catching a creature, bigger and meaner, in the wild? I am going to include snowman-guy catching on my F**k-It List.

DRIVE A RACE CAR IN THE INDY 500

I'm guessing at one time or another, regardless or your sex or age, every person who gets behind the wheel of an automobile, has had the uncontrollable urge to; 'put the pedal to the metal'.

We've all seen movies, whereby some criminal outruns the cops, and whether we want to admit it or not, we root for the criminal.

We think it's way cool how one guy in a fast car can outrun several cop cars coming from him in all directions. And, when he finally has caused the destruction of all the cop cars, and eluded them, we say to ourselves, "That's cool. I'd like to try that".

All the above, is for the most part, illegal. However, if you want to drive fast, and defeat other drivers, although they're not cops,(but you could pretend they are), you have to be a participant in a legitimate auto race. One such race is: the Indianapolis 500, held every year in Indianapolis, Indiana.

This race consists of drivers driving two-hundred laps around a track for a total distance of five-hundred miles, thus the name.

A lot of manly-type macho guys would like to partake of this event, but, I'm not one of them. I can see them liking the speed, and not having to worry about getting a ticket or some such thing.

However, when I see a car that's going two-hundred miles-per-hour, careening through the air, into the stands, or rolling end-over-end several times, and finally coming to a stop and bursting into flames, that has a tendency to dampen my enthusiasm for driving in the Indy 500.

If I want to be in car that goes fast and at the same time, risk my life, I'll just get in a car with some woman driver. It doesn't get much riskier than that.

Or, I could go to one of those arcades, and drive one of those virtual racing cars, without any threat of injury whatsoever. However, driving in the Indy 500, speeds onto my F**k-It List.

DONATE A BODY ORGAN

I hope if I ever need some sort of an organ transplant, there will be a long line of ready, and willing, donors. However, donating one of my organs to someone else, especially a stranger, is another matter entirely.

First off, what if the person I was donating to, was someone I really disliked, and, had for quite some time, wished they would die. Then, I find out that they were dying, but because I donated one of my organs to them, they will live for many more years.

I don't know if I could live with myself, if that sort of thing happened. Especially, if I just had a short time to live, depending on the organ I donated.

Regardless, organ donating is a risky business. Most people donate kidneys, because we have two of them, and apparently, we can survive on only one.

That would lead me to believe that we had the second one as a back-up , or spare, much the same as the spare tire in a car.

I can see a person donating their organs when are on their death-bed, or comatose, and have left instructions to do so. Here though, you'd be relying on people you trust, and they are few and far between.

I tell a member of my family that in the event I am in a coma or vegetative state, that they have permission to authorize to have my organs removed. What if they were the ones who needed an organ, or perhaps, wanted to sell my organs on e-Bay? I could maybe just have a touch of the flu, and already someone on the other side of the world is offering a family member some big coin for my compassionate, caring heart. Perhaps my family member made a deal to trade my liver for the front grill of a '56 Cadillac, he was restoring.

If I donated a kidney, it would be just my luck that while going through the operation, my good kidney would get infected, and I'd have to be on a dialysis machine for the rest of my life, while some sonofabitch is walking around with my good kidney, skit-skatting and chilling out. That wouldn't work for me. Therefore organ-donating goes on my F**k-It List.

WALK THE GREAT WALL OF CHINA

First off, The Great Wall of China, deserves its title. This wall is not just a,' fair' wall, not just a 'good', wall, but, truly, a 'great' wall, in every sense of the word.

But then, what else would you expect from a country that has hundreds of millions of Orientals, with lots of time on their hands? And, they must have had a lot of time, as it took eighteen-hundred years for them to build it, although, that time-frame involved many generations.

Construction was started in the seventh century BC, if you can believe that. Which makes the Wall around twenty-three hundred years old.

The Wall is over thirteen-thousand miles long. That in itself would preclude me from walking it, as thirteen-hundred feet would have me gasping for air, and pulling a ham string. You've got to ask yourself; "Who measured this thing"? I mean, someone had to walk the length , with a super long tape measure to perform this feat. Not?

I give the Chinese credit. They are essentially saying to their neighbors, and enemies; "We don't want you on our land, so stay on your own side of the wall, and, we'll get along just fine".

At any rate, there are adventurers all over the world, who want to walk the Great Wall, albeit, not the entire length.

Nixon once visited the Wall in 1972, and it's rumored he said; "Mr. Chinaman, tear down this wall". But, as stated, that's just rumor. As far as I know, the Wall's still there, probably attributed to the fact the Chinese didn't care anything about what Nixon said, as he screwed them on the trade deal.

So, if I decide to traverse the Great Wall, it will be by sitting in a rickshaw, being pulled by some Chinese coolies. After all, they built the damn thing, and, if they want me to see it, they can put forth some effort. Other than that, *walking* the Great Wall of China, is going on my F**k-It List.

RIDE AN ELEPHANT

The main problem with tourists is; once they get to a foreign country, they act all touristy.

Being in a foreign land, offers all sorts of adventures, that tourists would not normally see at home. Thus, I'm guessing, is the reason they go to foreign countries.

In foreign countries, what might be daily events, to the locals, can usually be quite an adventure to visitors.

Going to Asia or Africa, can offer a whole host of events, common to the general populace as normal, but, to the tourist, a once-in-a- lifetime experience. In both Africa and, Asia, riding on an elephant is a daily occurrence. They do this as part of their livelihood. However, to a tourist, this is a unique experience.

I suppose if an indigenous person from Asia or Africa, came to America, and took a ride on an escalator, they would look upon that experience as similar to an American riding an elephant.

Elephants can be very unpredictable and moody, and, on many occasions, have gone, 'rogue'. Especially, if they're having a bad day, and hate tourists and foreigners, riding them. Should this be the case, I would not want to be on their backs.

Why tourists want to ride a animal that is foreign to them is beyond my comprehension. I doubt if you'd see someone from Sweden going to America and wanting to ride a wild boar or an alligator. That just wouldn't make sense.

Elephants can be as dangerous to the locals as they are to foreigners. And, there is no way you can convince me, that some skinny Indian kid, using a bamboo stick, can control a rogue elephant, I don't care how much experience he has had.

If I'm riding a Shetland pony, and it goes rogue, although I have never heard of this happening, I'm pretty confident I can handle it, or, at the very least, jump off it, and, possibly outrun it. Even if I was a part-time animal trainer, and Ninja, I'd still avoid a mad elephant. Therefore, riding one of these huge beasts, goes on my F**k-It List.

TAKE UP YOGA

When I look at people who do yoga, I see
people who are very dexterous, agile, young,
and without proper goals in life.

I'll admit, I've watched videos of people, and
I'm speaking now of, foxy-looking babes,
doing yoga in leotards, and, for the duration
of their exercise, my eyes did not stray from
my TV screen.

I become somewhat transfixed whenever I
see a good-looking babe in leotards, doing
all sorts of contortions on a mat. I'm sorry,
but, that's just the way I am.

This is a practise, or exercise, inspired by
people of a different culture. The Dalai
Lama types. People will concentrate, on
exercises and, as they see it, exorcize all the
bad demons from their body and mind.

If I'd be into exorcising demons, the yoga
thing could be the route that I'd probably
take. If I were into exercising for physical
sake, ditto.

However, as with any exercise, a person has to be disciplined, and put a lot of effort into it, and, therein lies the problem with me.

I have no problem putting my efforts into such things as; beer drinking, polka dancing, eating, or anything that will make me feel good, but, exercising in general, and, yoga in particular are not goals I've set for myself.

How can I possibly try to manipulate my body into various contortions, when I have a hard time bending over to tie my shoes?

I don't understand yoga people. What are they trying to prove? So they can contort their body in all sorts of positions. Can they change a transmission in their car? Can they skin and gut a wild moose? I doubt it.

So, what advantage in life do they have that the rest of us don't? Sure, they are more physically fit than I am, and could beat me in a physical fight. However, if I ever had a confrontation with one of them, I'd just hit him or her with a big stick. End of story, end of fight. Therefore, I see no need for yoga, and, I'll put it on my F**k-It List.

TAKE IN FOSTER KIDS

There are a lot of orphans and displaced children out there, and there are a lot of people and organizations who take them in and give them a stable environment.

That is good. There are people out there, other than myself, or, in place of myself, who help the less fortunate in life.

Taking in foster children is akin to renting something like a house or car. You're not quite ready to buy yet, so until you decide exactly what you want, you rent.

People take in foster children, knowing full well that the children will be there for only a certain period of time, then they will be adopted by some loving, caring couple. A couple, who are obviously the complete opposite of the foster couple.

Taking in foster kids has an advantage over adopting, as; you will always be getting 'fresh' kids. If you have a foster kid whom becomes sickly, or eats too much, or gets smart-alecy, send him, or her back.

There are some reasons I'd take in foster kids, but compassion isn't one of them.

I would have no problem taking in foster kids, if I knew that they would stay until they finished all the chores and jobs I assign to them. However, if I take my time to train and teach them, and they leave in the middle of the job I acquired them for, I would be some upset.

It should be the option of the foster hosting family to decide which kids they want, and for how long. On a weekly or monthly basis, they should be able to go to orphanages or child welfare agencies, and pick through the kids they want.

Foster kids could shovel the snow, mow the lawn, do all sorts of things around the house and yard, thereby saving me some serious coin. However the coin I save has to outweigh the cost of feeding and clothing the foster kids, otherwise, I can see no reason for taking them in. Perhaps, if I could hire them out and keep the money, I'd look at that. Otherwise, taking in foster kids would be on my F**k-It List.

JOIN AA

I really don't know what the definition, or
the dividing line is, between being an
alcoholic and a drunk.

I recall that someone once said that the
difference between the two, is; that drunks
don't have to go to all those damn meetings.
That works for me.

I like my beer, and, on occasion, the odd
shot of whiskey. Beer, I pretty much drink
on a daily basis, unless, if I'm in a hospital
having some sort of major surgery, and will
be there for several days, or otherwise in
some sort of coma, and not having direct
access to beer,(unless they give it to me
intravenously).

However, first and foremost, I am not a
joiner. I am extremely averse to joining
clubs, organizations, clans, cliques or
anything under those umbrellas.

If I'm going to join any type of organization,
I want to know who they are. I don't want
them using aliases.

If I have an alcoholic sitting beside me, I want to know his name. With exceptions such as; the C.I.A., the K.G.B. or MI6, no one uses an alias, if they are on the up-and-up.

I don't fully understand the concept of Alcoholics Anonymous. What you have is, a bunch of people sitting around telling you how much they drank, how much they want to drink, or how much they're going to drink, once they get out of the damn meeting.

What do I care if some loser falls off the wagon and spends his mortgage money or rent money on booze? Unless, of course, he takes me to the local tavern and buys all the rounds.

Yeah. That's what I want to look forward to every week; getting out of my comfy Lazy Boy with a beer in my hand, and driving to some classroom filled with people who have all sorts of problems in life. If I wanted to do that, I'd just hang around with street people.

I'm going to drink to putting joining Alcoholics Anonymous, on my F**k-It List.

TITHE TO A CHURCH

I have a policy that when I go to a restaurant, I tip the waiter or waitress ten-percent. There are various arguments out there as to the percentage of the bill, that is a good tip. However, as I see it, a tip is a gift, and it should be my choice what to give. Truth be told, I have to give nothing.

All that aside, I tip because the server is usually making a low wage, and, likely as not, been courteous to me, at least he or she was, up until the time they see my tip.

At any rate, tithing is a common practise among church-going folks, regardless of religious denomination. Usually this amounts to ten-percent of a person's yearly income, which is generally dispersed over the course of fifty-two Sundays, as with Christians, attending their respective services.

Tithing is a practise I am somewhat on the fence on. Probably leaning to the side of the fence that doesn't tithe, or, tithes sporadically, and in differing amounts.

I fully understand that churches and other places of worship need money to function. If I were a regular church-goer, which I am not, I would look at the amount of time I spent inside my hallowed intuition, and tithe accordingly.

Say I was a Catholic, and went to mass every Sunday. A mass generally lasts one hour, and the most I will get out of it product-wise, is a wafer, called a host, which I'm guessing costs less than a penny, even in today's' dollar. Not even a shot of wine, to wash the host down. Therefore, I am getting little in the line of material goods.

There are 8760 hours in a year, and in a year I would, hypothetically, spend fifty-two hours in a church. That hardly justifies ten-percent of my income, as, I don't spend ten percent of my time there. And, it doesn't cost any more to operate the church, whether I'm there or not.

So, rather than go into a bunch of math and semantics, I'll just put tithing to a church, on my F**k-It List.

GO ON A BLIND DATE

At this particular juncture in my life, I am married, and, as such, would doubt very much if my wife would allow me to go on a date, blind or otherwise. She's funny that way.

However, if I was a single man, I cannot really see me going on a blind date. I would think that with all the online dating services, blind dates would be all but obsolete.

I can envision myself in a hypothetical situation, whereby some character I know, wanted to set me up on a blind date. The first thing he'd tell me is that she has a, 'nice' personality. That usually means she's a mutt.

When a person is willing to go on a blind date, that tends to tell me something about that person. She, as would be the case here, must have some problems, otherwise, she would have no trouble getting a date.

As far as myself goes, I would only be doing such a thing to help out a friend, or, otherwise act as though I was a decent sort of person.

I suppose there is a chance that a blind date could turn out to be some fox, but in my case that is about as likely to happen as me winning the lottery.

Some would look at going on a blind date as an experience, or even a adventure. If I want either, I'd either go skydiving or hunt grizzly bears.

I'm at the age in life whereby if I got a blind date, it would be that literally. Meaning, the woman would be old enough that she had used up all her eyesight, and was now legally blind.

We'd make a fine couple. Me half deaf in one ear, and her, blind in one or both her eyes. We'd go out to dinner, and through the whole evening, she'd be yelling at me, so I could hear, and I'd be feeding her as she couldn't find her mouth. What a sight that would be. If I made the wrong move, her seeing-eye dog would probably take a chunk out of my leg.

For the time being, at least, a blind date, goes on my F**k-It List.

HOST A NEIGHBORHOOD BLOCK PARTY

Neighbors are people, not unlike your working mates. You don't get to choose them, they're just there, where you are.

There's an old saying; "Good fences make good neighbors". I would add to that; "Good neighbors make good strangers."

Meaning, just because I live beside someone, doesn't necessarily mean I want to associate with them, or even get to know them, beyond saying; "hi" every once in a while.

Some people, especially in larger cities, hold block parties. They invite everyone on their block, to a street gathering. They will set up tables, have hog dogs, soda pops and beer, and things of that nature.

The reason being; they want to get to know their neighbors. I'm guessing these block-party hosts came either from a small town, or the country, whereby they knew all their neighbors, by default of size and numbers.

136

Likely as not, the neighbors they had in their small town were quite similar to themselves, in social status, job status, race, religion, and things of that nature.

However, in a larger city, such as; New York, for example, a person will get a whole mix and menagerie of people. Which is not a bad thing, it's just that you may not have as much in common with them as you would people in a smaller town.

Regardless, some people feel it's important, even essential, to meet their neighbors. I'm guessing mainly for security's sake. If you go out of town, you can have a neighbor keep an eye on your place. So, meeting and knowing your neighbors has some upsides.

However, those are outweighed by the downsides; you may not get along or agree on anything. Maybe your neighbor has kids or animals. Maybe they borrow and don't return, or, while you're away, break into your house, steal you blind and blame it on some street thugs. Therefore, hosting a block party to meet my neighbors is high on my F**k-It List.

FURTHER MY EDUCATION

As people get older, and hopefully more independent, financially and otherwise, they sometimes want to achieve a goal they had set early in life, but never accomplished.

One such goal, many people have, is to further their education. Get that college degree that eluded them for so many years.

Sometimes they want the degree to go back to work, or start another career, or further themselves in their present career situation.

Regardless, continuing a career in later life can sometimes be a daunting task. First and foremost, since a person has not been in school for many years, many things in life and science have changed.

Job descriptions have changed and many have even been eliminated. Because of technology, new-type jobs that were not even in the market before, have now sprung up.

That technology thing, it can be very technical.

I actually enjoy learning new things. I like taking little correspondence courses. I guess these are all signs of maturity and becoming interested in the world, and what goes on around me. Not

When I was in grade school, I hated it with a passion. Never paid attention, as my grades proved, and, just couldn't concentrate. In general, I looked at school as a waste of my valuable free-play time.

However, once I got into high school, I enjoyed it more, as the teachers and the courses were interesting. Although, I never did gain Rhodes Scholar status.

Now, I have three-score and six years behind me, and although I listen to the news, spend countless hours on my computer, I still don't know if I 'd want to devote the necessary time to studying.

To me the satisfaction of achieving a university certificate is outweighed by the fact I still like to have my free-time. What would I be anyway, a rocket scientist? We've already got an abundance of those. Smartening up goes on my F**k-It List.

BECOME AN ACTIVIST

The term, 'Activist' usually refers to people who protest, and volunteer, for projects that will benefit mankind.

That, in itself, would probably be my first reason, not to become such a person. What do I care about mankind? Mankind has never cared about me.

Activists will devote a lot of time, energy, and sometimes money, to causes they believe in. If any of those causes have ever benefited me, then I 'm glad they participated, and want to thank them for it.

As often as not, being an activist can get you in trouble with the law. It seems no matter what you're protesting, or endorsing, the law is going to be against you.

How often have you seen people in a peace march, who were set upon by the police? What's the deal there? Had the protesters stayed at home, there would have been no problem. But, they decide to congregate and march through the streets.

The next thing you know the bricks, stones, and Molotov cocktails are flying. And, this is at a peace march. Imagine the chaos and damage if they were proponents of violence.

There's no doubt that activists have made changes in the world. My biggest problem is; I don't know what I'd be an activist for, or against, as I dislike the way things are going in this world, as much as I like the way things are.

To go out and march would be something I'd do mainly to upset the status quo, and cause trouble. I'd look at it as an opportunity to be somewhat of a radical, yet at the same time, being admired for it by my peers.

Who wouldn't like to firebomb a building, burn a police car or bring a city to a stand-still for a day? I dream about that sort of thing. However, I would not want to pay the consequences for it.

Perhaps, if I could be an Activist, against Activists, I could get on board with that, as I'd be killing two birds with one stone. Otherwise, being an activist, has to go on my F**k-It List.

141

BREAK A GIUNNESS WORLD RECORD

We're all familiar with the 'Guinness Book of World Records'. If you're not, the title should be self-explanatory.

A lot of people go to great lengths to get their name in this book. They will literally risk their lives, to break a record, just so they can garner a few lines in the famous tome.

As for me, I am more considerate. If some damn fool, went through all sorts of pain, sacrifice or what have you, to break a record, or achieve a certain goal, who am I to rain on his, or her parade?

I've no doubt, if I really wanted to, I could break all sorts of world records, being it the person to make the fastest ascent of Mount Everest, to going over Niagara falls, not just in a barrel, but in a kiddies' wading pool, wearing only water wings. Whatever.

However, when I broke things as a youngster, I received a reprimand from my parents, so I learned my lesson.

Why a person would risk life and limb to perform some feat that would get them in the Book, is beyond me. Why not just bribe the Guinness' people, to put your name in?

When you get right down to it, who really knows who did what and broke some record, and got his or her name in the Book? More importantly, who really cares? Off the top of my head, I can't think of one single person who has his, or her name, in the Book. Nor do I care.

I could do record-breaking things all day long. The only thing holding me back is; fear. Also, how would the outrageous or dangerous feat I accomplished, enhance my life in any way?

The one exception I can think of whereby I'd like to have my name in, 'the Book', and would probably win, hands down, would be in some sort of beer-drinking contest. I'd shine in that one, without any effort whatsoever. But, as far as I know, that's not considered as a world-feat. So until it is, getting in the Guinness Book is on my F**k-It List.

BE A BIG BROTHER

The Big Brothers organization was first
founded in the early twentieth-century.
Some three-plus decades later, George
Orwell wrote his now famous novel
decrying 'Big Brother', singular, as a
'watcher' of society.

I think one can see the parallels here. On the
one hand, *the* Big Brother, is an entity,
literally watching the multitudes. On the
other hand, *a* Big Brother, is a single
individual, who has taken on the
responsibility to watch over just one person.

I'm guessing the irony is not lost on the
intelligentsia. It is quite possible, and, very
probable, that the Big Brother, in the
political-spy-sense, had a hand in setting up
the Big Brothers Foundation.

Think about it; prior to the advent of modern
spying and eavesdropping technology,
governments of any stripe, were reliant on
receiving information on possible dissidents,
from the latter's peers; common, everyday
working folk.

Brother would inform upon brother, wife on husband , sister on sister, grandpa on grandma, priest on member of his flock, and, so on.

George Orwell was certainly ahead of his time, and, as his novel has proven, many of his predictions have come to pass. However, I digress.

There are all sorts of, 'caring' types, if you will, who take it upon themselves to become a Big Brother. To help, assist, and guide, a younger person on the path of life.

I'm not one of them. If a young person wants to learn about life, let him sit in front of a computer screen, and learn it, as is the case with so many kids these days. Kids can learn all about what, famine, killing, wars, and, what have you, just by watching TV, and, doing the Google thing.

To me, those are the quick, and, best solutions. Why will I take time out of my busy, laying around, beer-drinking life, to help some stranger's kid. Being a Big Brother is big, but, not brotherly, on my F**k-It List.

CUT OUT BEER, TOBACCO, CHOCOLATE AND PASTA FOR A ~~MONTH, WEEK, DAY,~~ HOUR

Dieters, and Fasters, tend to make me sick. They have this notion that if they cut back on food, or refrain from eating certain foods altogether, they will be healthy.

What a misconception. These people watch Oprah way too much. And, speaking of her, the last time I saw her, she wasn't exactly svelte.

On a daily basis, either in some check-out stand magazine, or on some talk-show, you have people who have, or perceive to have, the answer to a healthy, long life.

In the words of Mahatma Gandhi, the Dalai Lama, and the Pope, 'bullshit.'

I've watched interviews of people who have lived beyond a century. Each and every one has a different philosophy. One will be a vegetarian, one will drink alcohol, and eat red meat every day, but in the end, what works for them is not the litmus test for life.

I don't know why it is that everything we like, in the food or drink department, is bad for us. For example; beer, tobacco, chocolate and pasta, are all, supposedly, bad for us. However, 'freak foods' like; vegetables, fruits and things of that nature are good for us.

Who came up with that? Why is it, with all the science they have in this world, they cannot put vitamins in beer and cigarettes? They could do it if they wanted, I'm convinced of that.

Why is it that only vitamins, vegetables and fruits the, called 'good' foods are the kind we have to force ourselves to eat?

Well,. I'm taking a stand here.. Perhaps I'll be alone, but, so be it. I want those damn scientists to forget about finding a cure for cancer or MS, and start working on how to make alcohol, tobacco, pasta and chocolate healthier. Do your job people.

Until such time that they do, I will continue to use, and consume, the above products. Refraining from doing so is so on my F**k-It List.

CONVERT A SCHOOL BUS INTO A MOTORHOME

Vehicle conversions have been going on for decades. A person buys a vehicle, doesn't like the way it looks, and does a complete remake, on it.

One popular conversion project is; buying an old school bus, and converting it into a motor home.

Admittedly, some of these turn out to be almost works of art, depending on how much time, money, and thought went into the project.

I know this all has to do with finances, as you can maybe convert an old school bus into a motor home, for less than half the cost it would be just to buy a motor home. But, in the end, you still have an old school bus.

Just borrow money from your family, friends , co-workers, or whomever, and buy yourself a motor home. Then, you'll be able to just drive away, from all those losers, who loaned you the money in the first place.

148

You might think that you're, 'uptown' meaning you have a motor home, but, that is just not the case. Sure, you can convince yourself, and your friends, that you are sophisticated, but, in reality, you're just some poor schmuck trying to pass himself off, as the elite.

An old school bus, is just that. No matter how elegant you make it out to be, it is, for all intents and purposes, an old school bus. A bus that was meant to haul a bunch of snot-nosed kids back and forth to school.

Show a little pride, for god's sake. Converting an old school bus is tantamount to wearing a tuxedo to a homeless convention. It just doesn't wash. I'd sooner steal a motor home than convert an old bus. That's just the kind of guy I am.

So, if you have an old school bus, start a school or something. Or, at the very least, pick up kids and drop them off in the forest. Just, don't convert a school bus into a mororhome. Please. This project goes on my F**k-It List.

BECOME A MALE-CALENDAR CENTERFOLD

No doubt there are a lot of womenfolk, although they may be up in years, who would like to see my semi-naked body on a calendar centerfold, if not on the cover.

I can fully understand that, as, I am what is commonly known among the elderly, and the dementia crowd, as a 'hunk.'

That stated, I cannot see myself flaunting my body. That's not me. I am a very humble person, and, although I am aware there are millions, if not thousands or even hundreds of women out there who would like to see me in a semi a natural state, it's just not going to happen.

I have a certain amount of pride, admittedly not a whole lot, but, a certain amount.

I don't like to tease people, I don't care who they are. So why would I tease some elderly ladies, possibly causing them to have heart attacks or strokes, just for the sake of getting world-wide attention for my physical looks.

Lots of men, mainly young hunks, like to pose for magazines, and show off their physiques for the ladies. I can understand that, as, I like it when hot babes do the same, so, I do not want to appear bias.

Even in my younger, more 'physically' fit days, appearing in a magazine or in a calendar was not my, 'thing.'

No doubt if I did such a thing, millions of copies would be sold, thereby making me very wealthy. Admittedly, for a brief, fleeting moment, I gave that some thought.

However, I prefer to keep my pride, and not make riches off my attractiveness, as it would not be fair, to the grotesque men who could never achieve such a goal.

'Pride goeth before the fall', as Napoleon or, Nietzsche, or Willy Nelson once said.

So, posing on a calendar, especially a centerfold, has to, for the sake of the faint-hearted women out there, go on F**k-It List.

BECOME A PEN PAL

A, 'pal', is a special individual. He, or she, is a person you like to chum with, communicate with, and trust.

In order for this to transpire, your pal has to, generally speaking, be in close proximity to you, physically.

Certainly, it's possible to have a pal, whom you have known for many years who moves away, and you're still pals. But, in that case, you became pals, by being in constant touch, geographically-wise.

Years ago, I don't know how long, nor who it was, someone came up with the concept of having a, 'Pen Pal'. Perhaps it could have even been two guys who shared a cell in prison, and corresponded upon their release. I don't know, that's just supposition.

How can you really call someone a , 'pal', if you've never met them? They can write what they want, but in the end, could turn out to be some freak you would never associate with on your worst day.

At any rate, somewhere along the line, the idea of corresponding with someone in another part of the country, or quite often, in another country altogether, seemed to intrigue people.

They could correspond with a complete stranger, and, over the course of months or years, get to know that person without having physically met them.

Every once in a while, these pen pals would meet in person. One would travel to the other's country, or vise versa.

Pen Palling was the precursor to Face book, Instagram, and other such social sites.

Even today, I don't use those sites for silly, mundane corresponding, as I don't care about anyone else's life.

I have never been a Pen Pal, nor intend to be one, as I don't need any more pals, especially ones with pens, or in the pen. Thus the Pen Pal thing will go on my F**k-It List.

TAKE UP JOGGING

Back in the Old days, if you were out
running on a public street, you were either
running to an emergency, or running from
the cops.

Back then, people did a hard day's work,
physically, and had no energy left to come
home and run. You got all the exercise you
needed at your job.

Nowadays, work is almost a euphemism, as
people may be employed, but, they don't
work in the literal sense. Meaning; exert any
physical effort, or produce brow-sweat.

Thus, they are out of shape, as is obvious,
when you go out and about, and see all the
fatties, and people who lose their breath
climbing up one flight of stairs, as is the
case with my own self.

In my day if you saw an overtly obese
person, likely as not, he or she had some sort
of a glandular problem, although it wasn't
known that well at the time. We just thought
people were fat, and oftentimes, teased
them, or at least talked about, and made fun

of them behind their backs, as we had little else to do back then.

Jogging has become an activity, if you will, that essentially involves the younger crowd, but, is not limited to them. Sure, you, see older folk out there jogging, if you can call it that, but not near as many as you will the younger folk.

And, as I have observed anyway, much to my delight, a large portion of the joggers are younger women, who want to keep their bodies toned, and, I am not opposed to that.

If I see a young buxom babe jogging by me while sitting on a park bench, I damn near get vertigo, watching her breasts bounce up and down. Sorry, but that's how I am.

At any rate, at my age should I take up jogging, the chances of my having a heart attack, outweigh the chances of toning my body ten-to-one. Even if I did lose weight, before that happened, the only upside for my family is they'd have to lay out less money for a narrower casket, and that won't help me any. I'll leave the jogging to the babes and put it on my F**k-It List.

WRITE A NOVEL

They say, (whomever, 'they' are, I haven't a
clue, and never met one person who was a
'they'), that everyone has a novel inside
them. Meaning, almost everyone, could
write some sort of novel, about something
they have experienced, or thought about in
their lifetime.

I am no exception to that rule. However,
writing a novel, and just thinking about
writing one, are two different things
altogether. I can think about dieting and
exercising, but, that will never happen , as it
is easier to think about such things than to
actually do them. Many great novelists, and
many, not so great, spend years writing a
novel.

'Writers block' is a ubiquitous term among
novel writers. This means that they come to
a point, and very often encounter this many
times, in the course of their writing,
whereby they cannot come up with any new
ideas to move their story forward.

I have enough trouble moving my life forward, and often encounter, 'life blocks' without getting myself involved in trying to write a novel, for which, I have no conception of an ending. Sure, I can start one, as I start many projects in life, being it cleaning the gutters or painting my den, but, it's the finishing part that's the hard part.

People seem to like stories that are gory and have sad endings, as opposed to stories that are just the opposite. Books by, or about serial killers, outsell books about people doing humanitarian work, and saving lives.

So, my ideal novel would be about joining a group of Christian humanitarians, who go to a Third-World country to help the less fortunate, then on their last day of work, the latter, would massacre the entire group of humanitarians.

That has the makings, and all the elements, of a guaranteed, 'bestseller', as, I've covered both ends of the spectrum. However, I can already see, that I'd have factions from both groups screaming for my head on a platter. So, I guess, I'll have to put novel-writing on my F**k-It List.

RESEARCH MY FAMILY TREE

Genealogy is a hobby many people, especially Baby Boomers, have been getting into.

They are not so much interested in where they are now, or where they are going, as they are in where they came from.

I suppose this has some merit. Providing you find out you came for good stock. However, what if you are a descendant of Vlad the Impaler, Stalin, or Adolf Hitler?

Would you then be putting that on your family tree collage for all the world to see? Or, would you, more than likely, be burying that somewhere in your archives and research files, and, end your search there?

Admittedly, I have some curiosity as to my ancestors. Do I come from royalty, I hope not. Do I come from a tyrannical family, again, hope not. If I come from average working-stock people, that will be fine with me.

Regardless though, the past is the past, and there's no unringing a bell. I can't see how my ancestry will change my life in any positive way, save for the fact; one of my distance relatives left an unclaimed fortune.

Should that be the case, I'd have to share that fortune will all my family and kinfolk, Providing, Heaven forbid, they did not all systematically befall fatal accidents, within days of each other, thereby leaving me the one and only surviving heir.

No doubt there could be a lot of interesting tidbits pertaining to a person's ancestry. One might find out that an ancestor was responsible for some great edifice or achievement, profiting all mankind.

However, even if that should be the case, I'd doubt very much, whether I'd gain, or benefit, in this day and age, other than a few lines on page six of a local newspaper.

As the saying goes; 'let a sleeping dog lie'. I think for me, the same will apply to my ancestry. Researching into it will have to go on my F**k-It List.

PAY IT FORWARD

Ever since the movie came out, by the same
name, as often happens with movies, life
will imitate art.

People in a drive-through lane at a fast-food
joint, getting a coffee and Danish, will pay
for the people in the cars behind them, as,
they want to, 'pay it forward.

To some folks, that will seem like a noble
gesture. Not to me. Some stranger, some
cheapskate is springing for a few coffees
and Danishes. Big whoop.

With my luck, if I paid it forward, there'd be
a hundred cars behind me, and they'd all
order Dom Perignon, and sirloin steak, as,
for that day, for one time only, this
particular joint has those items on their
menu as an anniversary celebration.

Thus, because I sprang for the cost, and paid
it forward, I'd possibly be forced to take out
a second-mortgage on my house, or, at the
very least, leave my car at the restaurant as
collateral for my bill.

Doing the Pay-It-Forward thing is an anonymous, and foolhardy gesture, to my way of thinking.

In the first place, how does a person know that the person they are paying-it-forward to, really needs it? I could be paying for Bill Gates' meal, for all I know. So, before I help anyone out, I want to know who they are, and if they are deserving of my kind gesture.

In the second place, what is the point in doing a kind deed anonymously? If you can't let people know you did it, and thereby brag, or otherwise, get accolades for your generosity, what's the point?

After all, isn't that what giving and caring are all about, so other people know you did those things. Who helps people out anonymously, and why? Not me, that's who not.

If anyone wants to pay something forward for me. go for it. I hope it occurs while I'm in a Cadillac dealership. But, as for me reciprocating in kind, it's not going to happen. Therefore, Paying-It-Forward goes on my F**k-It List.

TRAVERSE THE AMAZON RIVER
and TREK THE RAIN FOREST

The Amazon River, is the second longest river in the world, stretching almost four-thousand miles.

There are people who have made it a life's ambition, and succeeded, to traverse the entire length. First off, we're talking here about people who have a lot of time on their hands, and aren't doing this on a long-weekend vacation.

Even without knowing much about the river, or the journey down it myself, I'd guess that such a venture would be fraught with peril.

You have all sorts of poisonous snakes, man-eating piranha fish, alligators, insects, and naked indigenous tribal people. Okay, the latter may not be bad, unless of course, they're cannibals, which some are.

I don't see a venture such as this necessary, especially if you subscribe to the National Geographic channel. Those photographers, risk their lives, so I don't have to, and that works just fine for me.

162

As far as going to see the Rain Forest, I'm assuming, that you'd see it on your trip down the Amazon River, as would be obvious.

If that's not the case, you probably have to hike into the forest. A forest, no doubt filled with; poisonous snakes, insects and tribal people who may, or may not be cannibals.

And, what is the purpose of seeing the Amazon Rain Forest? Damned if I know. People just want to see it, as they think the day is on the horizon when it will no longer exist.

Apparently, lumbering corporations, as well as indigenous people are cutting down this forest at an alarming rate, both for the wood products, and clearing the land for planting crops.

Either way, here in North America, we have plenty of forest. Sure, a few bears and cougars to worry about, but not a real big threat. If I want to see trees, I'll stay here and look at them. Failing that, just go to an urban park, they have lots of trees without any dangers, save muggers. The Amazon thing goes on my F**k-It List.

163

ATTEND MY HIGH SCHOOL REUNION

A high school reunion is self explanatory, meaning; a meeting of classmates who have moved to different parts of the world, and never seen each other for decades, and are reuniting for 'old-times' sakes.

For; 'old times' sakes'. That in itself, to me anyway, is a misnomer. The truth is; people want to see how their old classmates' lives have fared in this world, as compared to their own. Has their life amounted to much, or are they just regular blue collar workers?

I personally know people who would go to a class reunion for the sole purpose to letting others know they have, 'made it'. In other words, became successful at one venture or another, via; luck, timing, or skill.

To me, I could care less whether my former classmates helped Bill Gates invent the personal computer, or are living on the street in a cardboard box.

The lives of old classmates, unless I was really tight with them while in school, don't have a lot of meaning, or concern to me. We each get one life, and, it turns out, how it turns out. Some people work hard and achieve goals, some inherit their fortunes, some get a lucky break, and still, some fall on hard-times.

I suppose it would be somewhat cool to go to a school reunion if I was the most successful person from my school. Especially, if I was a world-famous rock star, inventor or businessman.

Being the major achiever in the room, I could get a certain satisfaction looking down upon the failures, and semi-failures, who would be gathered there, and regale them with my tales of success.

However, if my worldly possessions are kept in the van, that I live in, down by the river, I may be reluctant to attend a high school reunion.

Thus, until I get insurance for my van, a class reunion is going on my F**k-It List.

STAR IN A REALITY SHOW

I abhor reality shows with a passion. To me, they have almost zero entertainment value, and, in reality, they are not reality, but rather rehearsed and scripted shows.

Yet, month after month, year after year, they garner a following, of what I can only perceive to be; people with EDD; Entertainment Deficit Disorder.

I can see watching a game show. at least it has some entertainment and educational value. But, a reality show. Give me a break.

I have no idea what type of reality shows are even on the television, and only get snippets here and there from articles I read about, or by channel surfing.

The Kardashians. Near as I can figure, they have no claim to fame, other than having a daddy who was one of O.J Simpson's lawyers. Talent eludes them, big-time.

There is a reality show where some bachelor or bachelorette will vie the opposite sex for their attention. Much like a farmer going to a cattle auction, and picking out the best hog, or heifer.

Dancing With the Stars. Yeah. that's a real nail-biter.

If I were asked to create a reality show, here's how my format would probably be: I'd have people taking all sorts of life-risking ventures, but, without any sort of safety net.

If they jumped from one building to the next and fell, they'd be toast. If they had to live with several other people for a specified amount of time, I'd have them eliminate their opponents, literally. If the contestants were on an island, that's where they would stay, unless they were damn good swimmers or boat builders. If you're going to make a reality show, make it a reality show. Don't wimp-out, with this Fisher-Price nonsense.

In the interim, unless someone offers me a real life-and-death show, the reality show business is on my F**k-It. List. If people can't be hurt or killed, what is the point of a reality show? Make it real, literally.

GO ON A HEALTH KICK TO LOOK and FEEL BETTER

Everyone these days from Oprah, to doctor Oz, to the Hollywood Beautiful people, are either on, have been on, are going on, or are promoting, a better health regimen. Likely as not, this will entail dieting and exercising. Pardon my crude, and vulgar language.

As people get older, they tend to be more concerned about their health, which to me is like the old saying; "what's the point closing the barn door after the horses have ran out."

Does anyone really think that for forty or fifty years you can laze around, drink alcohol, over-eat and then in your twilight years, you can reverse all that bodily harm by exercising, or eating better?

If I believed that, I'd have every piece of exercise equipment that's hawked on late-night TV. Plus, my cupboards and fridge would be stocked with bran, cereals, yogurt, vegetables and other such disgusting foods, people put in their bodies, without any hesitation.

168

Sometimes a person just has to resign himself to the fact that how he is, and how he feels, is as good as it's going to get.

Sure, there are band-aid solutions: hair color, makeup, clothes, crash diets. but these are just temporary. If for the better part of your life, you didn't take time to take proper care of yourself, chances are, in you later years, that's still not going to happen.

Eating and living healthy can be very stressful, and demanding. And, a person oftentimes has to change their whole lifestyle. The body just doesn't like you doing that, at least mine doesn't. I've tried changing to healthier foods and exercising, but my body told me to forget about it.

Your body is designed for you and only you. What another person's body will accept or allow, is altogether different from what yours will. If mine doesn't like rice cakes and dried fruit, I am not going to dispute that. My body knows what I want, and, has done so all my life. It tells me not to get stupid and healthy, and, I listen. Therefore, the health thing is way up on my F**k-It List, even if it kills me.

BE A GAME-SHOW CONTESTANT

There are some game shows out there that require their contestants to have a lot of knowledge.

Other shows require contestants to be spontaneous and hyper-active, as in jumping up and down, and yelling like a damn fool.

Some games shows, at least at one time, and I don't know if that still holds true, require a person to don some ridiculous-looking outfit, thereby not only humiliating the contestant, but, his or her family as well.

Then there are games shows whereby you just guess at multiple-choice answers and play with a group of people.

I have to admit, I wish I had the smarts to go on Jeopardy, and give any opponent a run for his or her money. But, the truth is, I can only get about one in four or five of the questions asked, on a good day.

After they come up with the correct answers, I always say to myself; " Damn, I was just going to say that", but, by then it's too late. I'm guessing if I was on the show, and said that, after another person had already answered it, that would not win me a plug nickel, nor garner me any favor with Alex.

I'd never want to be on any geeky show, whereby I had to show excitement, for being chosen to come up on stage, or even show excitement, if I won the prize. I don't like showing excitement, it doesn't excite me to do so.

I'd maybe like to be on that show; 'Who' Wants To Be A Millionaire'. What a dumb title. Who wouldn't want to be one, except maybe for a billionaire.

At any rate, I think going by some of the 'Millionaire' shows I've seen, I could probably get halfway through without a problem. Get up to maybe, fifty or a hundred grand. Then, if I had to call anyone for help, I'd want to call the guy who looked up all the questions, and has the answers that are on the cards. Of course, chances of that happening are slim to none, so, being on a game show, goes on my F**k-It List.

DO A RANDOM ACT OF KINDNESS

Meanness seems to take a front seat to kindness. I suppose this is just human nature. If two TV news station have on stories simultaneously, one about a mass murderer killing dozens of people, and the other about a kitten caught in a storm drain, we all tune into the killing story.

Which brings me to the complete opposite: a random act of kindness. This kindness thing is practised all over the world, and, usually goes unreported unless it has some unique significance.

There are all sorts of individuals, we periodically hear about, who will do a random act of kindness, just out of the goodness of their heart. It might be in the form of: buying a homeless person a meal; helping an old lady across the street, whether she wants to go or not; or dropping some coin in a beggar's cup. Whatever.

A *random* act of kindness, somewhat implies to me, that the kind person, isn't necessarily kind, and, may never be again.

However, this one particular time, they acted randomly, and were kind while so doing. And, someone was randomly there to record it, and, it made national headlines.

I don't know if I have it in me to do a *planned* act of kindness, let alone a random one. Random, is quite similar to spontaneous, and if I am going to be spontaneous, I want to plan it out.

Random acts of kindness are, for the most part, done to, or for, some stranger. How do I know that that stranger would appreciate a random act of kindness? Maybe he or she dislikes both random acts, and kind acts, and if I do a random act of kindness for them, I am committing a double whammy.

You never know if that stranger is going to fly into a rage and want to do you harm. Maybe he or she, just likes to be left alone. The stranger may be a person who commits random acts of violence, and you just lit his fuse.

I think being kind randomly, is okay, providing, it's not me doing it. Therefore, it belongs, randomly, on my F**k-It List.

BUILD A FORT

What civilized, red-blooded kid hasn't either built a fort, or wanted to build one?

It doesn't matter if it's a snow fort in the winter, or a tree fort in the summer, or, even an indoor fort during a rainy day, made out of couch cushions and blankets, a fort is a fort.

Inside your fort, no matter what it's made of, you have a sense of security. Yes, admittedly, a false sense, but, a sense none the less.

Nothing, nor no one could touch you while you were inside your fort, even your wimpy older siblings, who were no match against your wit, and twin cap six guns hanging from your waist.

The pillow, cushion, blanket, inside the house fort, was just a precursor to the one you envisioned in your mind, just as soon as you got your hands on some tools and building materials. Plus, of course, a few of your buds to help, with the understanding they had partial, limited access to your fort.

It's funny, how, as a person gets older, there are some dreams they want to fulfill, even though those dreams are, at this stage of life, bordering on infantile.

Case in point: a couple who have a large family, and a house bursting at the seams, saying someday they will get a bigger house. Then, once the kids all leave home and the couple has the money, they sell their current house and build a bigger one. But now there's just the two of them, the kids hardly come home, and the house is too big to keep up, so they sell it.

Same goes for a fort. Now that I'm retired, have the skills and the money, I really don't have that much need for a fort. The only person I have to hide from is my wife, and if she really wants me, she'll find me even if she has to wreck my fort to do so.

If I built a fort, my friends probably wouldn't come over unless their wives let them, and if they did, instead of fending off bad guys, we'd probably all just fall asleep. So, unfortunately, building a fort at my age, is going on my F**k-It List.

BECOME A VEGETARIAN

Animals were not put on this planet, just for pets, or for peoples' amusement, such as in zoos or parks.

No. Animals, meaning some, but not all, were put on this earth for man to eat. Be it; barbecue, roast, fry, sauté, or what have you.

There are those, and there seem to be more and more of them, or at the very least, they make the loudest noise, who believe animals are not for human consumption, and we should all be eating fruits, vegetables and plants.

These people are called; 'Vegetarians'. And, if they aren't bad enough, there is a radical version of them called; 'Vegans'. The latter, not only don't eat animals, but any product from animals like: eggs, milk or butter.

I dislike Vegetarians with their smug attitude. They were raised by parents who fed them meat products all their lives, and they ended up healthy. Now, that they've gone to college, smoked a few joints, let their hair grow, they have all the answers.

How many tens of billions of people have been eating at; McDonalds, KFC, and Burger King, to name a few, who are alive and kicking today?

Probably, worldwide, trillions of dollars have changed hands with all the meat-serving restaurants in the world, and they employed directly and indirectly millions of people.

How can vegetarians top this? Sure they have a few restaurants and stores around, but, what do they contribute to the economy, a lousy hundred bucks a year?

Just how long do people want to live? So a vegetarian, possibly lives to be ten years longer than a meat-eater, which, by the way, is not a fact, but supposition. Then what? If his or her friends are all carnivores, then, according to the vegetarian, their friends will all be dead ten years before they are, and they'll have to spend the next ten years alone. That crap doesn't wash with me, and for sure, becoming a vegetarian is on my F**k-It List.

SING CHRISTMAS CAROLS TO SHUT-INS

Someday, I might be a shut-in, and, if that day comes, I'm hoping everyone else will be shut-out. In the meantime, shut-ins are exactly where they belong, shut in.

Come Christmastime, people get all filled up with that Christmas spirit thingy. During the rest of the year they're just normal, old, introverted, selfish individuals. But once the tree and the lights come out, they go through a metamorphosis, and get the 'love' feeling for their fellow man, all through their body.

Naturally, when a person feels a certain way, he or she reacts accordingly. So, when people get the 'Christmas' feeling, they act all loving and caring and Christmasy.

They'll say and do things they wouldn't normally say and do. They'll say nice things, even to folks they don't like, and they'll do nice things for complete strangers. It's surprising how that Jesus' birthday thing has an effect on people. Come my birthday, no one cares diddly-squat, as it should be.

People do all sorts of giving and volunteering during the Christmas holiday season, as well. They will give gifts and meals, and volunteer at homeless shelters, and serve meals to the street people. The same people, by the way, who they pass everyday on the street without giving them a second look or thought.

Another thing some people do is; they go around to places where people are shut-in such as; hospitals and seniors' home and sing Christmas carols.

Likely as not these carolers have never sang together before, so they sure as hell don't sing in the same tempo. And, being as how they don't carry instruments, sing A cappella. This has disaster written all over it.

In the first place, I don't go around from place to place singing for strangers. I don't care who they are, or what time of year it is. If I did, I'd sure as hell want to do some rehearsing first, and be backed up by some rockin' band. But, since all that takes away from the spontaneity and goodwill spirit, I'll just put singing Christmas carols to shut-ins on my F**k-It List.

FORGIVE MY ENEMIES

'Forgiveness'. that's what the Bible tells us.
"Vengeance is Mine", sayeth the Lord.

This rhetoric is all fine and dandy, providing
you're the Lord, but, if you're just a common
pilgrim schmuk, it doesn't work out quite so
well.

If someone crosses me, or cheats me, the
first thing I want is revenge, and I don't
particularly care in what form. So long as
the aggressor suffers.

If God had not wanted us to take revenge,
then why did He come up with the concept,
or even the word, for that matter?

If people didn't take revenge, where would
this world be? If one country attacks
another, and the attacking country goes
unpunished, then it would attack all the
countries on the planet.

You have to have revenge. It's a necessary
part of life, as police, jails and prisons will
attest to. Of course, it's better to be the
avenger than the avengee.

180

I'm not really that much into forgiveness. That's not to say I don't believe in it at all. Should I do some harm, being it physical or emotional to another party, whether by accident or deliberate, I'd hope they would forgive me.

However, if the same should be the case with someone harming me or disparaging me in some fashion, I doubt if I could be quite so forgiving, nor, would I want to be.

"Revenge is a dish best served cold", as the saying goes, and, I can relate to that in spades. If you exact revenge on someone immediately after they have slighted you, you could face some serious consequences, depending on the actions you took. However, if you let the incident go by, and take your revenge weeks, months or years down the road, no one will suspect you, and you will probably get away scot-free.

I, for the life of me, cannot think of one single reason I'd want to forgive my enemies. That's why they're called enemies, because they're against me, and I don't like them. Therefore, I'll put forgiving enemies on my F**k-It List.

181

DO A HOUSE EXCHANGE WITH A STRANGER

Exchanging, is a concept that has been around for some time. I am mainly referring here to student exchanging, whereby a student from one country, will go to another country to live and learn, and vise versa.

However, house and apartment exchanging have only really come into vogue within the last ten years or so. This is a practise whereby, if you have a house in Toronto, and want to spend a month in Paris, then a person in Paris will come to live in your house for a month, and you will go there to live in theirs.

Not a bad idea, on the surface. However, your house, or apartment is essentially your sanctuary, and you are going to be giving it up for a period of time, to a total stranger, not knowing a single thing about them.

Sure, there are various screening companies out there that will vouch for, or otherwise, screen, a potential candidate, but this is not always one-hundred per-cent foolproof.

I don't keep money, jewellery, or anything of great value in my home, thus, robbing me, wouldn't be of a great benefit to anyone. However, as with most people, I don't like the idea of total strangers sleeping in my bed, using my bathrooms, kitchen and den.

Why would a person give up such a private thing just to save a few bucks is beyond me. If I did such a thing, likely as not, I'd have hidden cameras all over the house, as many people may very well have.

That would be another concern of mine. If the house I was living in for a few weeks, was rigged with all sorts of recording devices, and the material collected would show up on YouTube a week after I got home.

I could just see all sorts of people e-mailing me, and telling me they saw videos of me on YouTube, in various states of dress and undress. Maybe drinking milk from the carton, smoking cigars in the bedroom, and snooping through the home owner's private drawers and closets. Doing a house exchange; on my F**k-It List it goes.

PICNIC IN CENTRAL PARK

I've never been to New York city, let alone
Central Park. However, I've heard plenty of
horror stories about the latter. Not that it
isn't a fine park, I'm sure, it provides
solitude and happiness to countless urban
dwellers, who might otherwise not see green
grass or trees.

I've seen various news and documentary
film clips about, and of, Central Park.
Apparently it is used for; jogging, having
fun with the kiddies, lazing around and
picnicing. All the reasons why a park is
constructed.

I'm sure New Yorkers relish in the fact that
at the end of a hard work-week, they can go
to Central Park and kickback.

But, periodically, and, unfortunately, instead
of kicking back, some people get their backs
kicked, meaning; beaten and mugged.

Parks are not only for the regular,
outdoorsy-type folks, but, a prime spot for
the undesirable elements to ply their trade.
Meaning robbers and muggers.

I don't know if the relaxation factor is a good trade-off for the mugging factor. After all, a person can basically relax anywhere, even in your own home, and there, at least, your chances of getting mugged are almost nil.

New York being the largest city in North America, will no doubt, as with any city, have mostly good people. However, with the good, some bad comes along. What do I care if twelve million plus of the citizens are good people. My concern is running into or encountering just one bad guy.

As I understand it, New Yorkers aren't too quick to come to the aid of someone getting mugged, or otherwise set upon, by some nefarious person or persons.

Thus, I'm assuming, that if I were picnicking in central Park, and was being attacked, I'd be on my own. So, unless if have a contingent of New York's Finest surrounding me as I sip on a glass of wine and eat a sandwich whilst on a blanket in Central Park, that venture will have to go on my F**k-It List.

GET A MASSAGE

Getting a massage is pretty common with a lot of people. Indeed, my wife, gets one on an almost weekly basis. As for myself however, I have never had one, nor do I intend on getting one.

Were it not for the fact it is called a; 'massage', technically speaking the practise is no more than a stranger rubbing you all over your body.

These days, if some stranger even accidentally touches another person, say on a subway or bus, they can be charged with assault, or, a fight ensues.

Much the same scenario as a man running down the street in casual clothes, people think he is guilty of some crime and running away. However, if he's wearing a jogging suit, no one pays attention. I suppose, for any purse snatchers or muggers out there, who want to avoid getting caught, perhaps you people should invest in some jogging attire with money you made from your last mugging or purse snatching.

In order to give massages, a person; masseuse or masseur, female and male respectively, must take a course, and obtain a license.

So, based on that, if I take the training, and obtain a license, should I not be allowed to go around rubbing women's bodies, and get away with it? Seems to me like I should be able to. And if some woman complains, and calls a cop, all I have to do is show my certificate and license, and I walk. However, I'm guessing that wouldn't be the case.

Were I a masseur, I'd open up a shop that strictly caters to attractive babes. I don't know what fee would be fair to charge, but, I'd be willing to pay fifty bucks to every woman who lets me rub her down.

Getting back to the subject at hand; my getting a massage, I am very uncomfortable with someone touching my body. Not that my body is any work or art, but, it's mine and I don't think I 'd like anyone, especially a man having his hands all over me. It seems somewhat perverse. So, a massage will be added to my F**k-It List.

TAKE UP ART

For some reason, as people get into retirement age, they decide to take up art as a hobby. They'll be sitting in parks, or in the countryside, with their stool and easel, painting people, buildings, cows, trees and things of that nature.

I can't speak for anyone else, but, art is not just something that is a natural talent for most people. I, for example never got beyond drawing stick men, and even at that I suck, big-time.

I suppose it's okay to take up drawing and painting strictly as a hobby, and when your project is done, give it to a friend or family member. They can store it in a closet for years, then, at some point, chuck it in the garbage, where, more than likely, it belonged in the first place.

Art, as they say, is in the eye of the beholder. To me that's somewhat of a euphemism for; "what the hell is that supposed to be? A damn monkey with one arm could paint better than that. How is that art?"

I'm not what you'd call an art aficionado, but, neither am I some ignoramus. When I see someone waste paint, and a perfectly good piece of canvas, to paint a bunch of squares, circles and squiggly lines, I'm not impressed, nor fooled.

You'll see some hoity-toity come along and marvel at the depth of the painting and, comment on the bold brush strokes, and the kaleidoscope of color. But, what they are really saying, is; "I have no idea what the hell that is. My kid could do that, and he's retarded, but, I'll impress these peasants next to me with my apparent insight of talent this artist possess."That doesn't fool me for a minute, a piece of crap is just that, I don't care who did it. I like art such as: the bull dogs playing pool. Now that piece of work has meaning and character.

I can find so many things to do to occupy my time, that I will not try to pass off my stickmen art works as masterpieces. I have all sorts of talents; I can drink half a dozen beer without urinating. Now, *that's* an art. So the art/painting thingy goes on my F**k-It List.

BECOME A BORN-AGAIN
CHRISTIAN

There's nothing wrong with being a
Christian. I'm one. Maybe not so much a
practising one, but, one none the less.

Just when the; 'born-again' aspect of
Christianity came into being, I haven't taken
the time to Google it up. But, I do know,
born-again Christians are coming out of the
woodwork.

And, for all sorts of reasons. Perhaps they
did a stint in stir, and have now; 'seen the
light', and want to spend their remaining
days, following in the path of righteousness,
and spread The Word of Jesus.

Some become 'born-again' as it will further
their political, social, or business career, if in
fact they are looking for like-minded people
to support their particular calling.

I don't believe that, 'born-again' is just
something that happens out of the blue, by
having some sort of epiphany. No, it is a cry
for help.

There are things in life we will repeat over and over again, as it gives us pleasure, entertains us, or, otherwise enhances our lives.

However, some things should be just a one-time thing, and being a Christian is one of them.

What does that mean to be 'born again'? Does it mean that prior to that time, you were wandering around in a daze questioning your faith, or Jesus? And, if so, how do you know this time around it will be any better? How can you be assured that the, 'born-again' thing will take?

Just how many times can a person be reborn? Once, twice? Does advocating you've been 'born-again', somehow raise you to a higher level, as far as your faith and commitments are concerned?

I don't remember when I was born, literally, but, once was enough. I don't have to do that again. The same holds true, for being born, religiously. Once, is enough. Thus, being 'born-again', religiously, or otherwise, is on my F**k-It List.

BUILD AN UNDERGROUND
NUCLEAR BUNKER

Back in the early sixties, especially during
the Cuban Missile Crisis, some people
started building what were termed; 'fallout'
shelters. These were underground bunkers
stocked with food and water, and other
provisions. Enough for your family for
several weeks.

Once the crisis was over, and several years
after, when the 'Cold War' was supposedly
over, people, for the most part, gave up this
practise, feeling they had nothing to worry
about.

However, there are still some people, mostly
referred to as; 'Survivalists', who still believe
that a, 'Day of Reckoning', is at hand, and
that there could be a nuclear holocaust.

Most of the world has learned al lot about
nuclear bombs and devastation since that
first threat. Back then, we, as kids in school,
were told if a bomb was dropped, to hide
under our desks. Yeah. That was sound
advice. Whoever heard of fire burning old
wood.

However, since then, we have all learned that there is almost no chance of surviving a nuclear attack. Even if a person does survive the initial attack, when he comes out of his bunker, there will be nothing left. No clean water, no food, no other humans, no flora or fauna, nothing.

So, what's the point? Seeking refuge in a bunker and coming out only to realize that you've only extended your life, and that of your family, for a few weeks, at best. That would be like; if you're in a plane that lost a wing at thirty thousand feet, and you jumped out so you wouldn't be killed in the ultimate crash.

I'm sure a lot of these bunker-survival people, probably even have cash stored in their bunker. Like, where are they going to spend it when everything, has been totally annihilated?

I think while these people are building a bunker, I'll just chill out, and, if we both survive a nuclear attack, once they come out of their bunker, I'll just mug them, and take all their food. So, for now, building a bunker goes on my F**k-It List.

193

TAKE A CPR COURSE

Quite a few occupations nowadays, require a person to take, or have some sort of, First Aid, or CPR training.

At one time this training was only required for people in the life-saving business, or, first-responders. However, all that has changed.

Whether you drive a school bus, work in some industrial plant, or deliver the mail, companies want you to be able to save a life.

Why? The planet is becoming overpopulated as it is. Millions of people don't have the basics in life such as; food; clothing; a roof over their heads; education, electricity, running water, and the list goes on.

We can't even take care of the people we have on this planet. So, if we come across someone who is at death's-door, for one reason or another, what's the point of saving him or her? Let's concentrate on solving the entire population problem, before, going out of our way for one individual.

I suppose, if push came to shove, I could save someone's life, depending on that someone, and the circumstances. For example, if it were some foxy babe, and I knew she'd be indebted to me for life, that's a possibility I wouldn't rule out.

If I happened to be near some rich multimillionaire, and he had a heart attack, and I knew that saving him would end up by him rewarding me big-time, that could be another reason.

But short of important reasons like those, I think I might be somewhat reluctant. To administer CPR, you have to get on your knees, as the victim will be lying on the ground. What if I've got a new pair of pants on? Am I going to risk getting them dirty, just to save some stranger's life, who I might end up not liking once I've done so?

To take a CPR course, takes not only time, but money. If I take it, and save someone's life, should I not be able to charge for my services, or, at the very least, be reimbursed for the cost of my course? That probably won't happen, so therefore, I choose to put a CPR course on my F**k-It List.

RENEW MY MARRIAGE VOWS

At the time of this writing I've been married to the same gal for two-score and four years. If you put that in Dog Years, as it sometimes feels like, that would work out to be three-hundred and eight years.

Now, needless to say, I have a pretty good wife. We've had our disputes over the years, but, because here in Canada, we have to keep our guns locked up, which allows for a fit-of-rage to subside, we've both gotten by unscathed.

When we got married, back in the early Seventies, as with any marriage ceremony, we took certain vows. Damned if I know what they were, as that was a long time ago. But, I took them, and figured that would cover me for the rest of my life with her.

So far it has. But, apparently, that is not the case with all couples. For some reason unbeknownst to me, after a period of time together, when couples achieve a certain milestone in their married life, they decide to, 'renew' their marriage vows.

Just what is that supposed to mean or do? I can see renewing an old house or an old car, but, a marriage?

Years ago you made a pretty big commitment, probably one of the biggest, if not in fact, *the* biggest you'll ever make. There was a lot to thinking and pressure but, you pulled it off. Why would you want to go through all that again?

That's like going to a dentist to get a root canal. You fear it, you dread it, but you do it, and get it over with, hoping it will be a one-time thing. Then a few years later, you have to go in, and have that same tooth pulled, thereby going through all that agony again. Why?

When you make your initial marriage vows, on the day of your wedding, it should be stipulated in writing, that those vows are for life, and should never have to be repeated, except with another partner. As a matter of fact, you should have to take a vow, vowing never to repeat your first vow. Marriage vow-renewing for sure is going on my F**k-It List.

LEARN TO ROLLERBLADE

I have to admit, rollerblading looks like it could be fun, and have some advantages, to boot.

The latter being; you could knock people over, especially the elderly, as you skate by them. You could snatch women's purses, and be gone before they even got a good description of you. If you wanted to do a drive-by shooting, but didn't have a car, you could do a rollerblade-by shooting. The list is endless.

I've been to Venice Beach in L.A., and watched, transfixed, as wave after wave of lovely, scantily-clad babes rollerbladed past me, whilst I was kicking sand in the face of some wimp, wishing I knew how to rollerblade.

Growing up in the frozen, barren prairies of Canada, it was almost mandatory that you went ice-skating. I never really found any joy in that, as it took, what seemed like a lifetime, to lace and unlace my skates.

Then I skated around in ass-freezing temperatures, for a lap or two until I had to thaw out. Aside for all that, I was never a very good skater. I fell down a lot, and, got knocked down a lot. Therefore skating was never my forte, or high on my list of actives.

Although rollerblading looks like more fun, and is done in warm weather on pavement, there is still a certain element of risk.

Falling and scraping a knee, arm, wrist or elbow. Falling and cracking your head. Of course, you can buy all sorts of safety equipment, if you don't mind looking like a Class-A dork.

As a person gets older their reflexes are quite a bit slower. They tend to gain more weight, and if they fall, can suffer injuries, that a young person could just brush off. If I fell while rollerblading, I'd hit the ground like a ton of bricks, probably break half the bones in my body, and spend a year in traction. Thus, taking up rollerblading, is going on my F**k-It List.

BECOME A NINJA

Ninjas are cool, at least, I think they are, as I've never seen one, nor know anyone who has. They dress all in black, which saves time and money on wardrobe decisions. Plus, black doesn't show dirt or blood as do lighter colors.

Ninjas never seem to talk. So, if I was in Ninja school, I'd be able to concentrate on my studies, without some classmate yapping to me all the time, about who he killed, or how good he is at sword fighting, or some other such thing.

People fear Ninjas. It would be pretty cool, going to some function, like a wedding or business convention, and having everyone cower as you walked by, allowing you to be first up at the buffet.

Ninjas are quick and move about unnoticed, and mostly unseen. How cool would that be? I could sneak up on all sorts of people, give them heart attacks and slip away before anyone saw me.

Those are all the good things about becoming a Ninja. Conversely, as with anything, there are also downsides. Ninjas have to go through a lot of training. Years of it. And, they do this in some Oriental country, and I'm not a fan of Oriental cuisine.

Ninjas must take many tests like: sneaking; leaning how to be silent; how to throw those star-shaped killing thingys accurately; how to fight several people at one time with a sword, and, be able to endure some excruciating pain.

I'm not even getting into the mind games they must learn like; sensing someone is coming before that person even leaves their house;. hearing a cotton ball drop on a pillow; smell a person from a mile away.

The part that scares me is; I'd only have a damn sword. What if I run into someone with a gun? And, all that training. What if I spend ten years training, then fail the course. I'll spend the rest of my life paying off that student loan. Thinking in a Ninja mindset, it's best for all concerned, if I put becoming a Ninja, on my F**k-It List.

RIDE IN A PARADE

Parades were cool when I was a kid. People up on the floats, would toss out all kinds of cheap candy, and I'd go running out, like some little street urchin, at great peril, competing against all the other kids, just for a lousy candy worth a penny that I could steal from my local Five-and- Dime, all day long.

Also, on the floats were all sorts of people in cheap, homemade costumes of various kinds. Some of these people did actual entertaining on the float, thinking they were in Carnegie friggin' Hall. Singing off-key and playing instruments out of tune.

Naturally, there were several marching bands at intervals in the parade, that would stop, if they got too far ahead, and run, if they got too far behind.

Clowns walking along, or driving in little cars, as well as cowboys and Indians on horses, were also part of the parade. Then, there were the celebrities, at least in their minds they were.

A given was the local mayor, usually looking like a damn fool in a top hat, and riding in a convertible, that had to be brought in from another town, as no one in our town had a ragtop.

There'd be machinery-dealers driving their combines and tractors. Big thrill. Like people from a farming community had never seen that shit before. When those came by, it reminded all the farm boys of work, they had to do after the parade was over, and they all fell into a deep depression, threw their candies on the ground and walked back and sat in their dad's trucks. Talk about raining on someone's parade.

At any rate, once I got older I thought about riding in a parade, maybe even being the Grand Marshall. However there were all sorts of setbacks I hadn't factored in.

I'd have to wave and smile, both of which I hated to do. I'd have to put on some fancy duds conducive to the theme. Screw that. I'd have to get up early, and would not be allowed to smoke or drink alcohol on the float. The latter two are the deal-breakers. Riding in a parade goes on my F**k-It List.

TOUR THE CONTINENT

I know of several people who have; 'toured the continent', as it were. They relate their experience, as if they were the first people to do so, and will go into detail about what each city and famous edifice looked like.

They spent all that time and money, and all I had to do was, 'Google' it, and I saw everything it took them a fortnight to see, in less than an hour.

However, being at a place in person, has a different effect. You can soak up the atmosphere and ambiance, when you are actually, physically at a place. I'll give you that.

That said, I looked at the big picture. I realized there were hundreds of places I haven't been to in my own country of Canada, nor in the United states. So, why the hell would I want to go to a foreign country to see what they had to offer?

People in Europe plan, and save for years, to come over here and see what I have in my own backyard. So, I wondered if an European vacation was a must-do.

I gave this all some serious thought one day whilst in a drunken stupor. I asked myself, well, I thought I did, but in my condition I couldn't remember my name, so I made one up, but the bottom line was; why go to Europe where there are all sorts of foreign people with foreign languages and customs? What was the point?

So,. big deal, they've got rivers mountains and lakes, I do to in my own country. So they've got old ruins. Who wants to see old ruins? I have no desire to see ruins, but, if I did, the ruins would have to be new, otherwise, forget about it.

I took various things into consideration: time and travel expenses, living expenses, currency exchanges, and the whole ball of wax. I didn't like all those foreigners in my country so why would I make a costly trip, to see them in theirs?

I think the best thing I can do right now, is put a trip to the Continent, on my F**k-It List.

EAT A CHINESE MEAL WITH CHOPSTICKS

I don't like Chinese food. It may be appealing to the Chinese, but not to me. It isn't just the looks of it, and the not knowing what I am getting, it's also the smell.

Of course, the Chinese don't have a lock on this. All Asian food, East Indian food, Malaysian, food and all similar foreign foods, have a foul odor to me. An odor that hangs in the air for days, and weeks on end. It gets into a person's clothes and permeates everything.

At any rate, if you go to a Chinese restaurant, they will probably give you the option to eat your food with chopsticks, instead of utensils.

I can see the Chinese eating their food with chopsticks. Hundreds of years ago, as they didn't know any better, and had nothing better to use. But, once the white man invented utensils, why didn't the Chinese change? Surely they can see how superior utensils are.

There are people, North American, European people, is what I'm referring to here, who will go to a Chinese restaurant and, attempt to eat a Chinese meal with chopsticks.

Two sticks, I don't care whether they're called, 'chop'; or not, are not meant to be used to eat food, especially slippery, runny , greasy food. Using sticks to eat food is just one step up from using fingers.

I would think the Chinese, as they're supposed to be intelligent people like Confucius, would adopt a Western-style of eating, once it was shown to them just how archaic and foolish their way was.

At any rate, if I am ever going to eat food using a stick, it will be a kabob. At least that way, the food is speared, and there is little chance of it falling off.

I've seen amateurs trying to eat with chopsticks, and it would be disgusting if it wasn't so laughable. I'm quite happy using a fork or spoon for eating my meals. Thus, eating with chopsticks will go on my F**k-It List.

SEARCH FOR JIMMY HOFFA

It's pretty much a given that Jimmy Hoffa isn't coming home. More than likely, he's been prevented from doing so, because of his demise.

It's not surprising that Jimmy hasn't been found, or disappeared in the first place, considering the company he kept. You just didn't cross the kinds of characters, he associated with.

Jimmy disappeared over forty years ago, while supposedly meeting some, 'friends' for lunch. Yeah, some friends they were. They probably not only stiffed Jimmy literally, but, for the meal-check, as well.

Ever since then, there has been all sorts of widespread speculation as to the; who, where, how, and why.

Various nefarious characters have come forward for time-to-time, claiming it was they who snuffed Jimmy. As well, various leads have been followed from people who claim he's buried here or there.

People have been going missing for many years. Two most notable, besides Jimmy would be; Amelia Earhart, and Glenn Miller.

Certainly all sorts of speculation abounded in their disappearances, however, they were both on aircraft over an ocean, and that leaves a lot of parameters for disappearance.

However, with Jimmy, he disappeared on land, in America, during daylight hours, from a public place. Needless to say, a little more intrigue in play here.

We've all heard stories about how the Wiseguys will dismember their victims. Hopefully the restaurant in question, didn't belong to the Mob, and Jimmy ended up in quarter-pounders, or in Family Meal deals for the next week.

At any rate, there have been a lot of people, more adept then myself at such matters, who have searched for Jimmy and failed. Even if I took up such a quest, and found him, for my own well-being I'd probably keep it to myself. So, I'll let Jimmy rest where he is, and searching for him will be going on my F**k-It List.

GO ON A FAST, OR, A DIET

Pretty much from Day One, when I was born, my parents fed me. Since then, I've been eating everyday without fail. Whether it's a habit, an addiction, or a necessity, eating has become a big part of my life. And, it's also making me bigger, literally.

Being brought up a Catholic, during the Lenten season, my folks would make us fast. I never understood that. What good was my going hungry going to benefit anyone? If Jesus fasted, good for Him. That was His choice, but, why should I have to?

Essentially, with fasting, a person is abstaining from all, or certain kinds of food, for a certain period of time. A certain period, unless it's under an hour, is too damn long for me. If all Catholics are following this fasting rule, then why are there so many fat Catholics?

My body tells me, via, internal signals, that it does not want me to fast, and, I am not going to argue with my body, as, I assume it knows best.

Dieting. This is a practise whereby you aren't fasting, but cutting back on, and changing, certain foods.

I don't know why it turned out that way but, it seems to me that all the foods a person is supposed to cut out, or cut back on, are the foods that taste the best, and foods a person looks forward to eating.

Chocolate and pastas, are high on my list in the latter. Why is it that spinach, Brussels sprouts, and turnips are not on the list of foods we should avoid?

What fool came up with the widely accepted list as to what foods we should cut back on or avoid? I'd guessing he probably owns some vegetable farms, or at the very least, has a large block of shares in them.

To me, food isn't just something I consume to sustain my life, it is also an enjoyment. Who would want fish instead of turkey for Thanksgiving? Who would want a fruit salad instead of chocolate cake for dessert?

Fasting and dieting are musts on my F**k-It List.

JOIN A CLUB OR A TEAM

I'm neither a joiner, nor a team player. As a youngster, my dad kind of forced me into hockey and baseball, neither of which I liked. I didn't care whether we won or lost. No. I only cared if I made the goal or homerun.

Which, I probably never did. There was no way I was going to pass the puck for some dumbass teammate to score a goal and take all the credit. If someone else was going to be the hero, he'd have to do it without my help. Thus, with that attitude, I wasn't the most popular player.

So what? Where does it say we, as human beings, have to associate in groups or packs? Sure, lions, wolves and many other animals do. They do it for safety, surviving, and hunting purposes. But, we as humans, can get by just fine alone.

Joining a club or team oftentimes is associated with your job, and workmates. They want to get a baseball team, a bowling team, or a football team together.

The way I look at it is; I see enough of these derelicts at work, why am I going to spend my spare time with them? Obviously, they have no life away from the office or factory, and thus want to share their mundane life with others and, I don't want to be included in, 'others'.

Perhaps, they don't get along with their significant other at home, have a bunch of unruly, snotty, noisy kids and have to get away. Perhaps they don't read books, or maybe don't know how to read. What do I care. I'm not their babysitter.

Joining a club is a big commitment. You have weekly meetings; then have to participate in some event or fundraising they plan. You have to socialize with all the members, even though you don't know them, and if so, probably don't care for them too much.

If I could possibly be a team-player without joining a team, I might consider it. If there's a club for only one person, I'm there. However, failing both those scenarios, I'm going to put team-playing and club-joining on my F**k-It List.

213

MAKE A SANDCASTLE ON A BEACH

I'm not a, 'beach guy' per se. I seldom go to the beach, and, if I do, it's solely to look at the babes in bikinis.

I don't want to lie in the sun, and get a sunburn thereby risking my chances of getting melanoma.

I don't want to lie on a towel, on the sand, and have a bunch of snotty little kids and older freaks, running by me, and getting sand in my beer.

I don't want to go to the beach and play volleyball, or some other such dorky game. Those games belong on a court inside a building, not on a beach. You don't see people playing golf or hockey on a beach.

When people go to a beach, they seem to spend time doing things that one would not normally associate to beach activity, as per the above mentioned events and sports. However, some people go to the beach to make sandcastles.

Making sandcastles. What a temporary goal that is in life. I say temporary, as any castle you make has a very short life span. What's the point? That's like washing your vehicle before you drive through a muddy field. A futile use of time.

I've seen some of the sand castles people make, and some aren't bad at all. However, after all the hours of work put into it, a simple wave, or some untethered kid, can come along and destroy it in less than a minute.

That would just rankle me. If I made a sandcastle, I'd want it to be permanent. Once I was finished, I'd want to cover it in a concert shell, or some type of lacquer, thus making it next to impossible to destroy. I'd probably solicit the help of an architect, and a master builder.

However, that route, might defeat the whole purpose of a sandcastle, meaning, for relaxation and fun purposes. So, until I see kings and queens on beaches, making sand bungalows, I'll put building a sandcastle on my F**k-It List.

MAKE A TIME CAPSULE

Time capsules are generally made by cities,
so that years down the road, the local
citizens can dig it up, and see what was
happening ex number of years ago.

It's interesting to see how life, and the world
has progressed and changed over a period of
time, and time capsules can give a look back
to years gone by.

All sorts of things are put into a community
time capsule; a copy of a certain bylaw;
photos of the people in power; notable
citizens' notes; and things of that nature.

Some families make their own, personal
time capsule, for the benefit of future
generations.

However, as for me, I'd probably be opening
up my time capsule a week or two after I
buried it, and, not be real impressed with the
changes.

Chances are, I'd have put something in there
that I need, like; my favorite pen, or lighter.
perhaps the combination to my safe.

However, even if I did have the discipline to bury a time capsule, and not look in it for years, or even in my lifetime, and leave it to my children to discover, I might have some trepidations about that.

Once you put something in, and leave it, or seal it in such a way it's hard to retrieve, there's no going back. I'd probably wonder and worry, that I put something in it, that I might regret down the road, so much so, I'd have an early heart attack.

So, to be on the safe side, I'd probably put in things that had no connection to me whatsoever. After all, who would know, especially if the time capsule wasn't opened for fifty or one hundred years?

I could put in a copy of War and Peace, and using computer technology, put my name as the author. I could put in a spent bullet, and claim it was the one I pulled out of JFK. I'd put in a signed nude photo of Marilyn Monroe. By the time I was done, there'd be some edifice named after me, that's a fact. However, all that would be lies, and if I can't lie and fabricate, what's the point? A time capsule goes on my F**k-It List.

RECEIVE A KNIGHTHOOD FROM LIZZY

Many years ago, when I was just a youngster, I'd go to the movies, and be in awe of some sword-bearing hero, who was knighted by a king or queen. Of course that was years ago, and was just fantasy.

Apparently, the royals, in particular Elizabeth, the Queen of England, or, "Lizzy', as her friends and I call her, still believe in such fantasies.

She will take it upon herself to, 'knight' someone. This entails her dubbing the recipient a knight, and, that person can henceforth, be addressed as, 'sir'.

We are now in the twenty-first century. Why is this fantasy nonsense still going on? Who, in their right minds, thinks that just because some old broad, who wears a crown, and lives an opulent life, off the taxpayers' dime, can make them into a, 'sir'?

Of what nonsense is this?

I could see in years gone by, a person being knighted for bravery, or some such thing, but, nowadays, any schmuck who has a reputation for any reason, seems to be a candidate for this title.

Case in point; Mick Jagger. He's been a druggie most of his life. Do the British parliament or the royals condemn him for this? No. Lizzy makes him a knight. as though anyone, with the exception of some Brit would address Mick Jagger as, 'sir'.

Me thinks that Liz wants to impress celebrities in the entertainment business. It maybe gives her that, 'Queenie' feeling. She has the power to give some famous person a title, thereby letting that person, and all the world know, she is more important, as she is the title giver as opposed to the receiver.

All I can say is; "Lizzy. Get your act together, you silly old bat. Barry's not amused."

I can't think of any award, I'd want less than a knighthood from Lizzy, that's just to King Arthuresque .Being knighted, for sure, goes on my F**k-It List.

RECEIVE ORDER OF CANADA

This is another award, which was actually
established by Queen Elizabeth in 1967,
and, given to anyone for almost anything.

That crazy Liz. she has so little to do with
her time, that she has to spend it coming up
with, and bestowing awards on anyone, just
to make it look like she really has a role in
life.

The Order of Canada, recognizes
outstanding achievement, and dedication to
the community and service to the nation.
And, that covers a wide field.

It recognizes people in all sectors of
Canadian society. Their contributions are
varied, yet they have all enriched the lives of
others, and made a difference to this
country. Yeah. Really?

Just what does that mean in everyday speak?
Peoples' contributions? If I invented a new
simpler device for castrating pigs,, could I
be a recipient? If I came up with a new
breed of marijuana plant, would that be the
ticket?

What happened to the days when people got awards who really deserved them? When people made sacrifices, and spent their own time and money, for the betterment of mankind, and thus got an award, such as; the Nobel Peace Prize?

When did all this triviality take hold, whereby anyone could get some sort of award for just being able to dress themselves or tie their own shoes?

I can't, for the life of me, see myself at some 'high-brow' government function whereby I would be awarded the Order of Canada, because I wrote some smutty joke or anecdote for the Prime Minister.

Even if I came up with a way to quell the fear of Mad Cow Disease by switching the x-rays of a mad cow with those of a politician, (which wouldn't really be of any difference), would I expect to get the award.

Awards, with a few exceptions, are vanity trips to me. So, I'll just take receiving an Order of Canada Award offered me, and shove it, on my F**k-It List.

ATTEND AN EXECUTION

In Canada, capital punishment has been abolished totally since 1998. Prior to that, since 1967, there was partial abolishment. Meaning; a person could still be executed for certain crimes, against certain people. Apparently, all lives are not equal up here.

Thus, if after 1998, a person wants to attend an execution, he will have to make a trip to the good old U.S. of A., as executions are still carried out there, especially in the state of Texas.

Now, I don't really know anyone in Texas, and, if I did, hope that he or she would not be on Death Row.

As I understand it, a condemned prisoner can invite a number of people to see him or her, being executed. What the reasoning is behind this, I haven't the foggiest.

Nor, could I guess as to the particular acquaintances he or she would want to invite, nor why. Perhaps people who never came to any of his birthday parties.

We've all seen movies, or documentaries of condemned people on their last day. First off; they will be given a ,'last request' meal.

(Although, I understand many prisons have cut this out. I can only imagine they look at it as a cost-cutting measure. Especially in Texas where they'd, no doubt, save enough money on prisoners' last meals, to put new furniture in the execution-viewing room. Why don't they just give the prisoner a last meal, laced with arsenic? That way they can avoid the whole lethal-injection thing? Kill one prisoner with one stone, as it were.)

Then, we'll see the prisoner being strapped to a table, various tubes hooked up to him, and then someone, perhaps the janitor, I don't really know, will press a button or pull a lever, and the fatal drug will be injected into the condemned person's body.

I've never watched anyone die, and, don't know how I'd handle it. Likely as not, while he's on the table about to expire, I'd be worrying about whether my parking meter was about to expire, or, if the executioner validated. Therefore, I'll put watching an execution on my F**k-It List.

PILGRIMAGE TO THE HOLY LAND

A lot of people, especially Christians, try to make it a point, to travel to the Holy Land, once in their lifetime. Much like Muslims travel to Mecca. I suppose if a person has been to Vegas, Disneyland, the Grand Canyon, and a host of other world-famous sites, wanting to go where Jesus hung out, could be a logical choice.

Trouble is; most of these Holy Land visits, entail going with a tour group, or, on a charter flight. I'd probably be overcharged, on the fare and package incidentals. Then, when I got there, some Jew would be selling Christian souvenirs and Jesus' trinkets, at inflated prices.

All these Jesus' tour-guide folks know that you will probably be there only once, and that you'll be willing to open up your wallet for all the sundries they have to hawk. Jesus' tourists can't skimp whilst in the Holy Land, as they feel God is watching them, and He may question them about their frugality someday.

I suppose it could be cool, if a person knew for a fact that Jesus, Himself walked in this spot or that. Maybe, He spent a lazy afternoon in a local tavern changing all the wine in to water just for the fun of it, and you could knock back a flask or two in the same establishment. Or, perhaps, the original manger is still there, and you could bed down there for the night.

Just where does the Holy Land begin and end, per se? Are there people out there who are scamming tourists, claiming that such and such a place is part of the Holy Land, when in fact, it just regular land, and, there's nothing holy about it?

Even if I should ever decide to go to the Holy Land, I'd want some guarantees that it was, in fact holy.

Otherwise I might just as well stay at home, get some holy water from the Catholic church, and sprinkle it around my land. Maybe, I could even claim my land to be holy, and charge people to walk on it. I doubt it. Just wishful thinking. Therefore, I'll just put going to the Holy Land on my F**k-It List.

BECOME AN ANIMAL WHISPERER

First, you had your horse whisperer, then, your dog whisperer. Now, apparently, there are all sorts of animal whisperers: wolf; lion; bear, even shark whisperers.

Who put this over on us, and when? Could it have been The Sundance Kid, just because he wanted to make a movie?

As far as I know, animals don't know any languages, and respond to commands phonetically, or with actions, expressions and moves. So, if a person whispers to them, what difference does it really make?

Why not yell? Even we, as humans, don't pay attention when anyone whispers to us, but, if they yell at us, we tend to listen. Which begs me to ask the question; why aren't there any animal yellers?

Is the whispering supposed to have some soothing, calming effect on an animal? What if the animal is hard of hearing? If you whisper, it sure as hell isn't going to hear you.

As I understand it, the whole premise of animal whispering is to calm, or tame the animal. So, based on that, if you can get close enough to any animal whereby it will let you whisper in its ear, without it attacking you, I'd say that animal is pretty much as tame and as calm as it's ever going to be, so it doesn't need any fool whispering in its ear.

Just what is it that whisperers whisper in animals' ears? The animal cannot understand human language, so the whisperer could whisper any damn thing into its ear. The whisperer could whisper to the animal that it was a foul-smelling, stubborn asshole, and the animal wouldn't have a clue, and, probably lick the guy's face.

A number of years ago that gorilla , Koko, was apparently taught sign language.That makes me wonder, how does a person know if an animal is deaf or not. He could be whispering and the animal couldn't hear a thing, not that it could understand it anyway. Perhaps, if an opening for a sign-language whisperer ever comes up, I'll toss my hat in the ring. Until then, whispering to animals will be going on my F**k-It List.

BECOME A REPO MAN

When people get behind on their payments to banks or finance companies, whether the loan is for; a vehicle, furniture, electronics, what have you, a repo man is sent to their place to repossess the goods.

More often than not, these repo men repossess vehicles. Needless to say, when these characters come around to repossess something, the party getting the item repossessed is none too happy with them.

The people blame the repo man, even though they, the customers, are the ones at fault for missing their payment. The repo man is just acting for the financial institution, and has nothing to do with the loan, nor the late payments, and doesn't care one way or the other.

Sometimes things can get pretty nasty. People will fight with, or otherwise threaten the repo man. He oftentimes has to be sly and quick, to repo a car while no one is around. Stealth and speed, those are his traits.

I've never had anything repossessed, but, if I had, I'd probably act like the majority of people. I'd take it out on the repo man, and give him as hard a time as I could.

However, if I was a to be a repo man, that would be an altogether different story. I'd expect people to be courteous to me, and surrender their vehicles voluntarily. If they didn't, that's when the fun would begin.

First off, I'd travel with a Rottweiler, and a Pitbull. I'd carry Mace, brass knuckles, a taser, and a blackjack. And those items are for the people who are cooperative. For the unruly, I'd have an array of other equalizers.

I'd follow the people, and do the repo at their most inconvenient and embarrassing time. Like if they were at a wedding or funeral, or dropping their kids off at school.

What a hoot that would be. Him chasing after me down the street, trying to get his car back, because his wife and kids are inside.

However, if he caught me, that could not work in my favor. So despite the perks, I'll put being a repo man on my F**k-It List

MAKE UP A BUCKET LIST

Ever since the movie came out, of the same name, a bucket list, has become a popular phrase in the English lexicon.

Essentially, a bucket list is; a list of things a person wants to do before he, or she dies. Things that they were always wanting to do, and never could. But, now, in later life, have both the time and money to do them.

Needless to say, different people have different items on their list, and, those items are varied and wide-ranging, going from the simple to the complex.

Who doesn't have a whole bucket of lists that they wish they could have accomplished, or still can accomplish, in life? No one has the perfect life, without regrets, and, or unfulfilled dreams.

We certainly can't change the past, and, we can't change our general makeup, at least not to any degree. We are who we are. So, perhaps we, in our later years, can do something, or several things to help make our remaining years, more enjoyable.

For my part, if I did make up a bucket list, revenge and extreme wealth, would probably be at the top, or, not too far down.

If I can't settle a few scores before I check out, what's the whole point of life? Obtaining a large sum of money, whether I acquired it legally or not, would be of no consequence to me, as long as I got it.

Being able to go to hospitals, or nursing homes, and visit with people whom I never really cared for and, who, for most of their lives were smug or smarmy. And let them see how physically fit I am, and that I can come and go as I please. Maybe hire some foxy escort, and tell them she's my new, 'Squeeze'.

There would be no boundary to my list. However, my biggest concern would be; that I'd go through all this trouble, spend a lot of time and money fulfilling my wishes, and, either get a stroke, or, get hit by a bus. Then, all would be for naught. Therefore, I'll put making a bucket list on my F**k-It List, and leave it at that.

www.ingramcontent.com/pod-product-compliance
Lightning Source LLC
Chambersburg PA
CBHW071525040426
42452CB00008B/890